The Anger Management Toolkit

The Anger Management Toolkit

Understanding &
Transforming
Anger
in Children &
Adolescents

HINTON HOUSE Therapeutic Resources

Sue
Jennings

HINTONHOUSE

Dedication

I am delighted to dedicate this book to my older son Andy Hickson, with whom I share so much about working with troubled youth.

Wolf drawings for Part 3 by Chloe Gerhardt
Other wolf drawings and worksheets by Suzanne Hall

Published by
Hinton House Publishers Ltd, Newman House, 4 High Street, Buckingham, MK18 1NT, UK
T +44 (0)1280 822557 F +44 (0) 560 3135274
E info@hintonpublishers.com

www.hintonpublishers.com

First published 2011
Reprinted 2012, 2014

Printed and bound in the United Kingdom by Hobbs the Printers Limited

British Library Cataloguing in Publication Data

A catalogue record for this book is available from the British Library.

ISBN 978 1 906531 31-7

Contents

Part 3   **Teenagers Aged 14–17 Years**

Part 4   **Resources**

List of Resources

Acknowledgements

I must thank Sue Hall for all her help and advice in producing this book, and the many groups of children and young people who have given me ideas and suggestions.

Friends and family have been very patient with my pre-occupation. Special friends in Romania and excellent students make my work there a joy.

Thank you Sarah Miles for being a lovely publisher with whom I work: we will meet in Malaysia soon!

And beloved Peter, my husband is always there for me and keeps feeding me when I forget!

Sue Jennings
Glastonbury & Zarnesti
2011

Introduction – Using The Anger Management Toolkit

This resource is a practical handbook of ideas and strategies for dealing with anger and aggression in children and young people. It seems to be a contemporary phenomenon that people express themselves through anger and intimidation, often in sudden outbursts. There is little 'Pause for Thought' (PfT) or opportunity for people to reflect on their angry feelings, before they react. There is a lot of anger expressed that seems to be 'Out of all Proportion' (OaP) to the initial offence, slight or frustration. This is what I describe as an 'action – reaction' approach. Often the reactions can be out of all proportion to the event itself. We need to remember that once feelings are aroused, logic goes out of the window, and this applies equally to young people and adults.

There will be teenagers who will try to sabotage practical approaches to their struggles, it won't be considered 'cool', and as for colouring pictures! This is why we have built in choices for as many techniques as possible, and a contract for group members to agree.

People talk about 'meaningless anger' or 'over-the-top' anger without any attempt to understand what has triggered such angry responses. We have new expressions such as 'road-rage', which have generalised into the word 'rage' being tacked on to many situations (shopping-rage, school-rage, telephone-rage). This may be a handy, if lazy, way of describing something, but it does not help us address the issues and detect underlying causes.

People will also suggest that it is the soft option to understand the why and the how of anger: 'She should show me more respect', 'My father would not let me behave like that', 'I blame the school – not enough discipline', 'I blame the parents – not enough discipline' …

Pause for Thought (PfT)

This book is written for teachers, therapists, psychologists, youth workers, care workers and parents, with the hope that everyone will 'pause for thought' to re-consider why children and young people are so angry and at times, so violent. Not only do I suggest that children and young people need to pause for thought, but also all the adults who work with them. Adults are as guilty of reactive behaviour as young people themselves. As we PfT, it is important to reflect that there is an alternative to having an 'action-reaction' approach, manifested in the 'misdemeanour – punishment' cycle. I think it is possible to develop an 'action – interaction' way of working where communication strategies are developed between angry young people and the adults surrounding them. If we can develop action and interaction, it will be possible to begin to shift stances that seem fixed and unyielding. It does not mean that we 'let people off lightly' or that we 'take the soft option'. What it does mean is that we try to discover ways of understanding the angry behaviour on the one hand, and find ways to change it permanently on the other. All statistics suggest that violence in young children will probably lead to violence in teenagers and then adults. Recidivism in all prison populations is not reducing, so it is obvious we need to re-appraise how we deal with anger and find new ways to manage it.

I have written elsewhere about changes in our language with the creeping in of violent expressions (Jennings 2011a). We 'kick-start' a meeting or a project or a programme; we grab coffee, food, bags of crisps; we could 'kill for a cup of coffee' … How many of these phrases do we use without being aware of them? There are also titles of books and organisations such as 'Beat a Bully', 'Beating Anger', countless games using terms such as 'Rage', 'Exterminate'. Perhaps a few pauses could encourage us to select phrases to use that are less combative and more engaging.

The PfT approach

This book proposes some alternative responses and ways of considering the underlying causes of angry and inappropriate behaviour. It provides a host of tried-and-tested techniques for addressing anger management in the age ranges of 5 to 8, 9 to 13 and 14 to 17 years. It also makes the point that our responses can be flexible and respond to the needs of an individual or group 'in the moment'.

The approach described in this book unpacks 'anger management' into several components: not only are possible triggers for angry behaviour explored, the accompanying feelings are also considered. For example, I have discovered that a lot of angry behaviour is masking fear. There are many scary and frightening situations, such as violence in the home, parental separation, sudden and unexplained deaths, that can result in children and teenagers displaying angry or violent behaviours. This can happen especially when being scared is considered weak, or children feel too vulnerable to show their real feelings.

Other children can be very angry under the surface but mask it with compliant and extremely controlled behaviour. This may be easier to manage but can result in nightmares, self-harming, eating complications or other self-destructive ways of being. The anger is being turned against the self, or used in extreme ways in controlling others. Whether we are discussing 'Out of all Proportion' (OaP) responses such as extreme rage that results in a trashed classroom, or multiple cuttings that result in blood loss and hospitalisation, the causes or triggers for the anger need be understood and new behaviours practised and performed.

OaP Responses

When as workers in the field we are confronted with OaP responses from children and teenagers, it is hard for us to stop our reactions escalating. For example, when teenagers are cruel to animals or brutal to their class mates, we can say things like 'How would you like it if you had your ears cut off' or 'I am going to do to you what you did to Susan and see how you like it'. It is almost an 'eye-for-an-eye' Old Testament approach that is only likely to escalate the anger and violence. When young people commit violence towards the more vulnerable, they have usually become inured to pain, and do not express empathy or remorse about what they have done. Therefore reacting with more violence will only compound the situation, and not address any understanding of the situation by the people involved. Of course crimes must be punished, with punishments that are appropriate to the incident, but should also be accompanied by the opportunity to change and re-learn.

How this book is organised

There are three parts to this toolkit that focus on three age groups: Children (5 to 8 years), Older Children (9 to 13) and Teenagers (14 to 17). In each part there are seven sessions that address particular themes as illustrated in the table below.

ANGER MANAGEMENT SESSIONS			
No.	5–8 Years	9–13 Years	14–17 Years
1	Introduction	Introduction	Introduction
2	On Fire	Exploding	Erupting
3	Worries	Nervousness	Anxiety
4	Teasing	Bullying	Intimidation
5	Muddles	Confusion	Chaos
6	Scares	Fears	More Fear
7	Ending	Ending	Ending

They are designed so that each session can be worked through in sequence during a seven-week programme (or a seven-day intensive course). Alternatively it is possible to choose particular sessions as a programme that fits the needs of a particular group or person. It is also possible to work across the age groups. For example, if a group is involved in major issues of bullying, it is possible to work first with the session on 'Teasing', then 'Bullying' and then 'Intimidation'.

Individual group leaders will know the level that is appropriate for their age group, and the following sessions have only a very general age guide. For example, there may be teenage groups that would benefit from some of the more pictorial exercises for the younger age groups. Some individuals who struggle with words, or have difficulty with expressing their feelings in words may be helped with the tick-box exercises. The important issue is that the group starts with a general introduction and ends with an integration of the programme.

Structure of Each Session

There are 21 sessions, with seven in each age range, and they follow a specific plan that can be built on and have a cumulative effect on learning and change.

Each session begins with a note of any **Preparation & Resources** needed, and the **Aim** and **Focus** for the group. Next is the **Warm-Up** before moving on to the main activities. The **Warm-Up** is both a preparation and an aid to group cohesion and collaboration. **Warm-Ups** serve as a channel for energy, to focus attention, and to allow bodies and minds to be stimulated for appropriate action. Every session has warm-up ideas and there are more in **Appendix 3**, if you need more ideas or want to replace any of those in the text.

The **Main Activities** give a focus for the theme in hand, and this may not be a direct way. For example, rather than expressing the anger about anxiety, it could be more fruitful to understand the anxiety and change that. The session can end with **Feedback & Sharing** and then the relevant **Story** as a closure exercise, and completion of the **My Progress Today** worksheet. However, sessions can be developed further using the **Worksheet** provided for each story. For the older age groups there are also drama and puppet worksheets. There is an extra story, worksheet and drama worksheet provided in Appendix 2 (Worksheets 13a, 13b and 13c).

WolfWork

The wolf is an important emblem throughout this book, and each session has a **WolfWork** worksheet. The wolf is important because of its many facets as well as the many misperceptions about what wolves can be or do. Wolves are family creatures and usually mate for life; they care for their young through extreme opposition, and role-model appropriate behaviours. However, there are also lone wolves who have deserted the pack and try to live life away from the others. Wolves have been perceived as violent, often gratuitously, and there are many campaigns to remove wolves as vermin.

There are no wolves in the UK but in Romania they are now a protected species. Sickly children in Romania used to be fed their milk through the skull of a wolf in order to make them strong.

Using the WolfWork sheets will enable young people of most ages to relate to this animal without feeling they are being treated like a child. The wolf provides a strong identity for children and teenagers of all ages, and is useful for crossing possible gender and ethnic divides.

It is possible to use all of the WolfWork activities as a progression in their own right, leading from the simple to the more complex.

Homework

Every session has a worksheet for group members to take away with them. It may be that it is more appropriate for this work to be done at the after-school club, or with an individual classroom assistant or learning mentor, or in a nurture group. The homework gives time for reflection away from the programme and to try and get feedback from other people, teachers, peers, parents, siblings, friends, and others at a sports club and so on. The more each individual can be sustained in making progress and bringing about change, the more the change is likely to be permanent. All the homework sheets can also be completed with drawing or with discussion.

Personal Journals & Diary Notes

Personal Journals are a way of re-cycling paperback books (also described as Altered Books, Thomas, 2011, for more detail search online for 'Altered Books') as a means of creating something highly personal and individual. Each group member is given a discarded paperback book (charity shops are always giving these away or selling them cheaply for a bagful!). Using an old book gives the existing book shape to work with, in terms of pages and cover. Inside it is possible to remove pages and replace them with new ones; one can write on the pages with thick marker pens; try cutting out a secret compartment in the middle, having stuck a block of pages together, in order to put inside something private such as a letter or a poem. Adults enjoy making these journals too. They can be added to each week, a cover created and ties made from wool or fabrics so they can be truly closed. Journals can also be made by using a blank book with thick pages that can take both writing and drawing, but I prefer the recycling approach. Journals referred to in this book are different from **Diary Notes**. Diary notes are for jotting or drawing anything that is not included in the Progress Sheets. For example, children may want to record their smiley faces or specific examples of things that have happened, and the more we can enable communication, the more understanding will increase. There is a template for Diary Notes, Worksheet 4, in Appendix 2, with other choices of worksheets.

Resources

It is really important to hold your group in a room where participants can move around, especially when working with anger management. Many of the participants literally need room to breathe and it is important that they do not feel crowded. If it has to be a classroom the chairs should be in a circle and not in rows, with easy access to materials and white board.

- A large white board and markers are necessary for use by the leader and participants. Where possible, try to write down words for reflection or ideas generated by the group. In addition, have to hand art materials including crayons and coloured pens, pens and pencils, blank paper, glue, masking tape, scissors and blades. Large soft balls, football size, can be used for many warm-ups and games.

- Small drum or tambour for keeping time.

- Old books for making journals, or hard-backed books with blank pages are important for recording feelings and ideas. Envelope-style folders are easier for younger children to manage and ring binders, with plastic pockets, are suitable for older groups.

- For puppet making: newspapers, masking tape, scraps of different materials, wool and ribbon.

- For collage work: old magazines and newspapers, large strong paper at least A3 size, pens and stickers for decoration.

Materials that can be recycled are a stimulus for creativity, so a box of scraps and junk, for rummaging, will assist this process.

Cautions!

It is important to remember that disturbing, abusive or painful information may be disclosed during this work. Some young people may use anger to cover up situations or events that they prefer not to think about. Any disclosures or information on worksheets must be handled with sensitivity and care. Please adhere to any child protection policy that is in place, or consult with whoever is overseeing health and safety, or social and pastoral care. Therapists will of course consult their own supervisors.

It is important to show care and support and not to react with shock, disbelief or disgust.

Just remember PfT and OaP towards all children, young people and adults!

Part 1

Younger Children Aged 5-8 Years

Session 1   General Introduction

What do I know about my anger?

Preparation & Resources: Folders, 'Angry Words' worksheet (Worksheet 3, Appendix 2), paper with large pre-drawn circles, and coloured pens, diary sheets.

Aim: To encourage understanding of the programme and participation, and that everyone experiences anger in different ways.

Focus: To allow everyone to have a voice and acknowledge similarities and differences.

Warm-Up: Ask everyone to run around, in and out of everyone else, with no touching: repeat it very slowly and then even faster. Invite members of the group to find a partner who is the same height; face each other, and one person is the mirror and the other is looking in the mirror; the mirror must follow the actions of the other person: combing hair, putting on makeup, pulling faces and so on; then change round.

Main Activities: Share with the group that everyone is valued as an individual, and encourage them to look at the 'Angry Words' worksheet:

- Suggest each member draws their angry face inside a circle.

- Then draw their calm face inside another circle.

- Which of the angry words describes their angry face?

More Advanced: In pairs, *with a basic rule of no laughing or teasing*, say one thing that really makes you mad.

Feedback & Sharing: Write on the board different suggestions of what makes us angry; invite everyone to put their portraits on the wall and look at similarities and differences.

Closure: Place portraits in folders, read the story of 'Leanne', complete the Story Worksheet, write Diary Notes (template Worksheet 4, Appendix 2) and complete My Progress Today.

Go to the Story Sheet and then WolfWork.

(P) This page may be photocopied for instructional use only. © *The Anger Management Toolkit*, S. Jennings, 2011

The Story

Leanne is angry because she finds it difficult ...

Leanne was just seven when she started her new school. She had come back with her mum and dad from another country where her dad had been working. Everything was strange to her: the weather was so cold, she didn't know the language very well, the lessons were very different, the school days were longer, and she had never taken a packed lunch or her own drinks to school before.

Some of the other children just stared, others laughed, and some were cruel and whispered things about her. The teachers sighed and thought "She will settle down soon, it will be strange at first".

Leanne was very unhappy and very angry with her parents for doing this too her, and she thought no-one at school liked her.

So Leanne decided she would be different in another way – she would try and make people laugh. She gave funny answers when the teacher asked questions; she cut herself a fringe that covered her eyes and she pretended she couldn't see; she did a funny walk once she got to school and lots more things as well.

What was going to happen to Leanne?

Story Worksheet

(Draw or write your answers)

1 Why is Leanne so angry?

2 Why does she find the schoolwork so difficult?

3 Think of three other things that Leanne could do to try and make people laugh.

4 What would you do if you were Leanne?

WolfWork 1

1 Wolf-cub will achieve something each week in the group. Draw or write by each rung what you hope to achieve by the end of the course.

2 Draw a picture in the circle of how wolf-cub is feeling now.

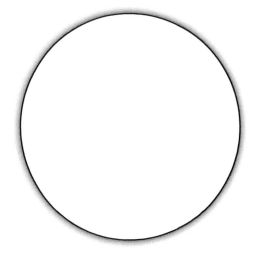

My Progress Today: The Face of My Anger

1 Colour in the face that shows how you are feeling now.

Not angry at all   A little bit angry   very angry

2 Have you ever felt angry because you feel different? Colour the circle to show how different you feel from other people.

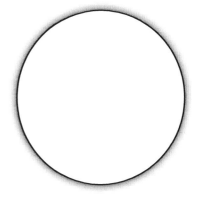

Very different   Quite different   A little different

Homework

Things to think about ...

1 What sort of things are difficult if somebody is different?

2 Does it really matter if some people are different from others?

3 Is it OK to be different in some ways but not others?

Perhaps you can share these questions at home or with a friend.

Maybe you would prefer to draw a picture; draw a portrait of any famous person in the frame below.

Session 2   Anger & Fiery Feelings

My anger feels like a fire!

Preparation & Resources: Poster(s) of camp fires, barbecues, small drum or tambour, folders.

Aim: To express and set limits on angry behaviour.

Focus: Discussion of fiery feelings.

Warm-Up: Encourage everyone to scatter round the room, running in different directions and stop when the tambour sounds one beat; start again with two beats; vary the pace until everyone can run around without colliding into anyone else, and then stop-start together.

Main Activities: Suggest that everyone looks at the fire pictures and thinks about how fire moves and the sounds it makes: crackling, hissing, popping; repeat the following sequence with stop-start on the tambour.

- Everyone moves just their fingers like flames.

- Everyone moves their arms and the fire grows bigger.

- Everyone finds a space in the room and makes a fire with their whole body, including noises discussed.

More Advanced: In pairs, create the idea of 'bursting into flames' and its sound together.

Feedback & Sharing: Encourage everyone to talk about where in their body they feel angry; maybe it is their tummy or in their chest.

Closure: Read 'The Fire Child' story, write Diary Notes and complete My Progress Today.

Continue with Story Worksheet and WolfWork.

The Story

The Fire Child

Once upon a time there was a child who was always known as the Fire Child. Fire Child loved everything to do with fires: the smell of the wood smoke, the crackling and hissing of the sticks, the dancing of the flames and the way the fire would glow like a fiery cave.

When the class were asked to draw a picture, Fire Child would always draw fires of different shapes and sizes. Large fires with flames reaching to the sky, fires that were small and glowing, fires in fire-places that you might see in houses, and big bonfires that are built for fireworks night.

One day at school, everyone was playing outside and Fire Child was chasing with a group of friends. Suddenly Fire Child stopped. Something was wrong, there was that smell, the smell of smoke, but where was it coming from?

[Invite the group to give suggestions of where the smoke is coming from, and encourage everyone's suggestions as possible sources of the smoke.]

Fire Child ran to the teacher and told her there was a smell of smoke. The teacher rang the fire bell, and all the classes and teachers came into the playground. The fire-engine arrived very quickly and found that the smoke was coming from the house next door. Someone had burned their cooking!

Fire Child was thanked by the teacher and the fireman for smelling the smoke so quickly. "You really are a Fire Child," said the Fireman. "Maybe I could fight fires when I am grown up!", thought Fire Child.

Story Worksheet

1 Draw a picture of a fire with lots of smoke.

2 Think of three fire words and write them down.

_____

_____

_____

WolfWork 2

1 Wolf-cub will achieve something each week in the group. Write or draw by the ladder what you think you have achieved and ask your friends and teacher to tell you too.

2 Draw a picture in the circle of how wolf-cub is feeling now.

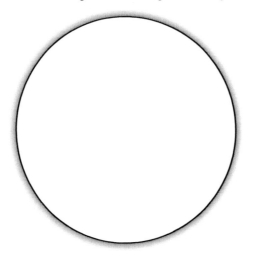

My Progress Today:
The Fire of My Anger

1 Colour the fire to show whether you were feeling lots of anger, some anger or only a little anger when you started today.

2 By the end of the session were you feeling:

 A bit more angry than usual?

 A bit less angry than usual?

 Just the same?

3 Do you enjoy watching fires?

Homework

Suggest that everyone looks for pictures of fires in magazines and comics and brings them to the next group. Remind them to get permission before cutting out pictures if the magazine belongs to somebody else!

Session 3   Anger & Worries

I am angry because I worry

Preparation & Resources: Pictures of multicultural and multi-ability groups of children; art materials (crayons, paints, glitter glue, paper).

Aim: To find ways for children to value themselves.

Focus: Discuss any thoughts and feelings from the previous session and share homework themes.

Warm-Up: Ask everyone to run round the room and remember how to stop at one tambour beat and start again at two beats; then stop at one beat and make a shape that is very tall, and then small, very wide and then very narrow.

Main Activity: Creating a Self-Portrait

- Invite everyone to think about portraits of people in magazines, famous people, school and family photographs.

- Encourage them to paint or colour a portrait of themselves.

- Make a frame round the portrait by painting or colouring: it can be a circle, oval, square or another shape.

- Suggest that everyone thinks of three good things they like doing and three things they don't like doing: they can write them down or tell the rest of the group.

More Advanced: In pairs, *with a basic rule of no laughing or teasing,* encourage everyone to share something that they worry about.

Feedback & Sharing: Why do people worry? Is it about being different and not like others? Are our families 'different'? Does it matter?

Closure: Read the story of 'Robin, Tom and the Green Snake'.

The story can be read as a closure story with no discussion or it can be followed with the story worksheet in this session. The questions can be discussed in the group, written down or drawn.

Write Diary Notes, and complete the WolfWork and My Progress Today.

The Story

Robin, Tom and the Green Snake

One of the boys at school was called Robin and he lived on a farm. He was having a tough time because he found a lot of the schoolwork very difficult. He had missed a lot of school because he was helping to look after his Dad who was ill; Robin helped with some of the farm work too. The other children teased him and called him bird-brain. Robin used to run home from school as soon as possible, but didn't say anything much to his parents, younger brothers and sisters or even his grandmother. He was not going to worry his parents with Dad being so ill. So he did all the worrying himself.

Although Robin found a lot of his schoolwork complicated, he knew more than anyone else about the countryside, wild animals and flowers and trees. One day a new boy, called Tom, arrived at the school. He saw that Robin was being teased, and knew that he was different too. Tom was only good at one subject and that was maths. He never needed a calculator because he could work out anything in his head, faster than anyone else, even the teacher.

On his way home after school, Tom saw Robin kneeling near a big tree at the edge of leafy path that would take him to the farm. He was watching something, very intently, in the grass. Tom could also see that two children from school were hiding behind the hedge, they were holding bunches of stinging nettles and he could guess what they were about to do. He went quietly up to Robin and knelt beside him; Robin smiled and pointed to a grass snake, sunbathing on a stone. The two watching children decided to creep away; they were not going to take on two strong lads. Tom watched with Robin until the snake decided to slither away. The two boys stood up and smiled at each other, and then went on their way home.

Story Worksheet

1 Why didn't Robin tell his family about the teasing at school?

2 What were the other children feeling about Robin?

3 What do you think Robin was feeling and not showing?

4 Would the other children start to tease Tom because he was different too?

5 What would happen next day at school?

6 Might something change now that Robin and Tom could become friends?

WolfWork 3

1 Wolf-cub will achieve something each week in the group. Write or draw by the ladder what you think you have achieved and ask your friends and teacher to tell you too.

2 Draw a picture in the circle of how wolf-cub is feeling now.

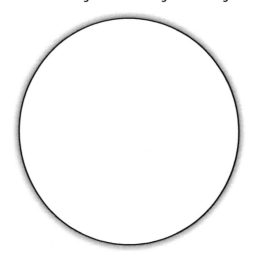

My Progress Today:
The Fire of My Anger

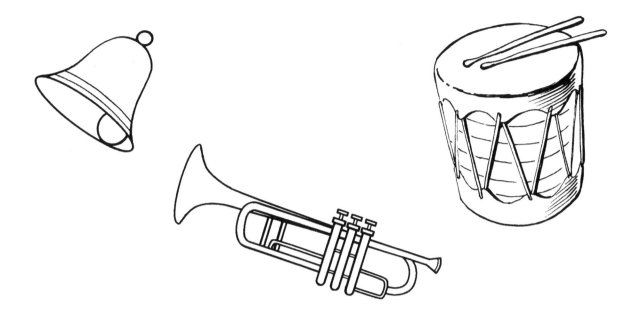

1 Which of these instruments would you play to show how you are feeling now? Colour your choice in with colours that you like.

2 Draw a cross on the line to show where you feel your anger is right now.

_____

Very Angry   Quite Angry   Little Angry

3 How did you feel about Robin and his being teased and bullied?

Homework

Things to think about, to write or draw:

1 What are the things that people worry about in themselves?

2 What are the things that people worry about in other people?

3 Who could do something about our worries?

If you can, ask someone at home or friends to help you answer the questions.

Bring your thoughts to the next session and draw a picture if you wish.

Session 4   Anger & Teasing

I am teased because I am different

Preparation & Resources: Posters of tigers, cats, sharks and dolphins.

Aim: To express and change an angry feeling and feel confident.

Focus: Discussion of the previous session and share homework themes.

Warm-Up: Ask everyone to run round the room and remember how to stop at one tambour beat and start again at two beats; then stop for one beat and create the shape of a tiger; start-stop again and create the shape of a shark; repeat the start-stop with a cat and then a dolphin. In pairs, ask the cats and dolphins interact, and then the other animals.

Main Activities: Develop the animal movements and the changes; narrate the following sequence to the group before inviting them to respond to it:

- Suggest everyone curls up and pretends they are a sleeping cat.

- Slowly they stretch and yawn and start to move round the room.

- Then they see a barking dog, and tense up and get ready to fight.

- The dog ignores the cat; the cat relaxes again, and continues moving.

More Advanced: In pairs, *with a basic rule of no touching*, explore other differences between people and how it feels.

Feedback &Sharing: Discuss in the group themes of differences.

Closure: Read the story of 'The Warrior Queen and the Tiger', write Diary Notes and complete My Progress Today.

Continue with Story Worksheet and WolfWork.

The Story

The Warrior Queen & the Tiger

In a faraway land lived a very strong Warrior Queen. She was young and proud and spent her time walking through the forests in the palace grounds, and following animal tracks. She never hunted the animals but slowly got to know them; she was very different from her father the King who always liked to go out hunting. One day she was following some interesting footprints in the mud, and almost tripped over a very large tiger that was lying quite still in the undergrowth. The animal growled and then whimpered and licked its paw. The Warrior Queen asked the animal to let her look at its paw and she found a huge thorn. No wonder the tiger was in pain! Quickly and firmly she pulled out the thorn, and the tiger yelped and then went on her way.

Some years later there was unrest and fighting in the land and some invading bandits had captured the castle and taken the Warrior Queen prisoner and tied her up. There were too many bandits for the Queen to fight and she felt helpless and alone. The next day the bandits were shouting and mocking and laughing at her, and saying that now she needed to try to be a warrior queen, because she would die in a fight. They took her to a big cage and pushed her through the gate.

In front of her was a large and angry tiger. The bandits had teased the tiger so that it was angry and ready to pounce. It came rushing towards her, showing off its enormous teeth and wickedly sharp claws. But the tiger stopped in its tracks as soon as it saw her, and gave a little whimper. It lay down at her feet and she stroked its head. The bandits were very surprised and suddenly quite afraid! They opened the door of the cage and ran away as fast as they could. The Warrior Queen returned to her palace and from now on had a very powerful guard!

Story Worksheet

1 Draw a picture of the cage with a very strong fence, where the tiger was kept. Draw the angry tiger inside the cage.

2 Think of three words to describe how you feel about tigers.

WolfWork 4

1 Wolf-cub will achieve something each week in the group. Write or draw by the ladder what you feel you have achieved and ask your friends and teacher to tell you too.

2 Draw a picture in the circle of how wolf-cub is feeling now.

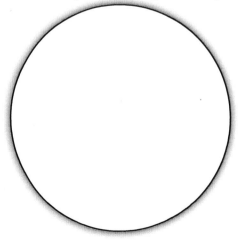

My Progress Today:
The Claws of My Anger

1 Colour in the tiger to show whether you were feeling lots of anger, some anger or a little anger today.

2 Colour in the circle of how you are feeling right now.

Very Angry   Quite Angry   A Little Angry

3 What did you feel about how the bandits treated the tiger to make her angry?

Homework

1 Next time you see someone being teased think about how you would feel if it was you.

2 What would you do if you were teased?

3 What might people tease you about?

If you can, ask someone at home or friends to help you answer the questions.

Bring your thoughts to the next session and draw a picture if you wish.

Session 5   Anger & Muddles

I am angry because I am muddled about my feelings

Preparation & Resources: Bundles of wool with several balls muddled up together, folders, paper and coloured pens.

Aim: To explore feelings of being muddled, and find some clarity.

Focus: Discussion of previous session and share homework themes.

Warm-Up: Run and freeze, run and form a feeling shape (lost, tired, angry, upset, happy), run and make a feeling face (scared, angry, pleased, lonely, happy).

Main Activities: To explore through drama games muddled feelings that may all be happening at the same time:

- Suggest that everyone works with a partner and give each pair a bundle of wool.

- Encourage them to work together to untangle the wool, think about how people's feelings can be like this too, all muddled up.

- Invite the group in the same pairs, to create a body sculpt that is like the muddle wool, all twisted and tangled (see notes on Body Sculpture in Appendix 3).

- Take time to slowly untangle the body sculpt and talk about how it felt.

More Advanced: In pairs, one person is the sculptor and the other the clay. Ask the sculptors to 'model' the clay into the shape of a feeling, and name it.

Feedback & Sharing: In the group discuss how people felt to make the different feelings with their bodies, and think about which ones are familiar and which are uncomfortable.

Closure: Read 'The Lost Dragon' story, write Diary Notes and complete My Progress Today.

Continue with Story Worksheet and WolfWork.

The Story

The Lost Dragon

Most dragons live in caves high up in the mountains and when they fly they go on long journeys over the woods and the seas, and they roar and breathe fire. However, people forget that dragons start as babies inside shells and that it takes time to learn to fly and to develop their beautifully coloured protective scales.

When Drag broke her way out of her shell, she was left to look after herself and she felt very muddled about her feelings: sometimes she was cared for and sometimes she wasn't. Some days her parents left some food out for her, but they were often away for a long time at night, and slept for most of the day. Sometimes they did not come back for several days as they had flown far away over the mountains.

Drag kept herself busy by exercising her wings every day and was developing a beautiful coat of pale and dark green scales. She looked out from the entrance to the cave, and decided she would try to fly to the next mountain. It was a bit scary, but … one, two, three, FLY! She took off and with a huge effort landed on a smaller mountain. Feeling very pleased with herself she took off again towards the next mountain, then again and again. Whew!

Soon she felt tired after all that flying, and decided to rest. She looked around. Drag had no idea where she was and began to feel scared. Where was she? What time was it? There were no grown ups around to help her. Just then, she saw a big dragon flying towards her, and recognised him as her friend's dad. He landed close by and told Drag that Molly had noticed she wasn't there and had been worried about her. Relieved, Drag climbed on to his back and he flew her back to the cave. Molly came over to meet her and asked if they could play together. Drag could only nod with pleasure; she didn't know what to say – no-one had ever worried about where she was before. Maybe one of the grown-ups could talk to her mum?

Story Worksheet

1 What do you think Drag was feeling when she was left on her own?

2 Why do you think she did not have other dragons to play with?

3 What might she have eaten as a baby dragon?

4 What does she need to do, now that she is back home again?

5 Will her parents do anything when they come home?

6 What should Drag tell them?

WolfWork 5

1 Wolf-cub will achieve something each week in the group. Write or draw by the ladder what you feel you have achieved and ask your friends and teacher to tell you too.

2 Draw a picture in the circle of how wolf-cub is feeling now.

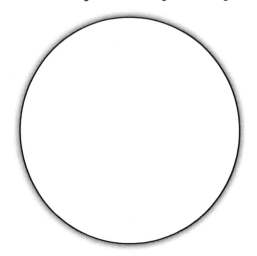

My Progress Today:
The Smoke of My Anger

1 Colour in the dragon to show if you were feeling lots of anger, some anger or a little anger today.

2 By the end of the session were you feeling:

 A bit more angry than usual?

 A bit less angry than usual?

 Just the same?

Homework

1 Think about any muddled feelings that you have and how they make you feel.

[ ]

2 What questions might you need to ask someone so that you feel less muddled?

[ ]

3 What is the strongest feeling you have when you are muddled?

[ ]

If you can, ask someone at home or friends to help you answer the questions.

Bring your thoughts to the next session and draw a picture if you wish.

[ ]

Session 6   Anger & Fear

I am angry because I am scared

Preparation & Resources: Posters of dolphins; lots of old newspapers, folders, paper and coloured pens.

Aim: To encourage trust of peers and overcoming fears.

Focus: Discussion of previous session and share homework themes.

Warm-Up: Hold hands in a circle, and try not to break the circle as everyone pulls in opposite directions; practice lots of different swimming movements.

Main Activities: Create the 'island game' with newspapers and then draw and colour individual islands:

- Place sheets of newspaper at intervals around the room to create 'islands'.

- Everyone must 'swim' around the room until a tambour beat and then occupy a newspaper island without tearing it – inevitably several people have to hold onto each other on one island.

- Ask everyone in the group to draw and colour a picture of their own island and what surrounds it.

More Advanced: Encourage the whole group to colour a large piece of paper blue, then individuals can draw their own islands to cut out and place on the 'sea', and then add any creatures that might be in the sea.

Feedback & Sharing: Share a description of your island with a partner and note anything they have in common.

Closure: Read the story of 'The Dolphin who Swam with Sharks', write Diary Notes and complete My Progress Today.

Continue with the Story Sheet and WolfWork.

The Story

The Dolphin who Swam with Sharks

It happened after the storm. A small dolphin called Greatly didn't know where he was; he swam in circles feeling very lost. Before the storm he had been with a group of dolphins, big and small, who were friends, and always swam together. They played games and chased each other, leaping into the air to test their strength, and seeing who could go fastest. Then the storm came.

It had happened very quickly, and huge waves carried away all the dolphins and scattered them in different directions. The big dolphins knew how to go with the waves, but the smaller ones did not have the strength. The waves carried them off and when the dolphins tried to surface, a howling gale blew them through the water and they could hardly breathe. When the storm eventually died down, the small dolphins were everywhere except together.

Just then, some sharks swam past and noticed Greatly swimming in circles all alone. "Hey!" they called, "Wanna come with us?" Greatly wasn't too sure, but they seemed to be friendly, even though they did look quite fierce. Shyly, he swam towards them and they bared their sharp teeth as they grinned at him. Greatly began to feel scared as the sharks seemed very aggressive. They snapped at passing fish, and even knocked some out with their strong tails. Greatly followed the sharks, but he was not happy.

Unknown to Greatly, his two special friends, Giant and Grand, had been looking for him. They had found each other after the storm but not their third friend. They had worn out their voices blowing their special whistle, hoping he would hear it. Suddenly, they were alert! Sharks were nearby! They sensed it using the special system that dolphins use for communication. The older dolphins arrived and found Greatly swimming among the sharks. The bigger dolphins followed the sharks at a distance, and let them know they were Greatly's friends; they were grateful to the sharks for taking care of Greatly until he found his family.

Greatly was overcome with joy to be re-united with Giant and Grand and they swam away together, starting to play their old games again. However, this time they did not swim too far away from the bigger dolphins – they needed to learn more about 'going with the waves'.

Story Worksheet

1 What might have happened to Greatly if he had not been rescued?

2 Why do you think his friends were called Giant and Grand?

3 How did they feel when they could not find Greatly?

4 Is there another way that Greatly might have been rescued?

5 Would it have worked?

6 What lessons has Greatly learned from this experience?

WolfWork 6

1 Wolf-cub will achieve something each week in the group. Write or draw by the ladder what you feel you have achieved and ask your friends and teacher to tell you too.

2 Draw a picture in the circle of how wolf-cub is feeling now.

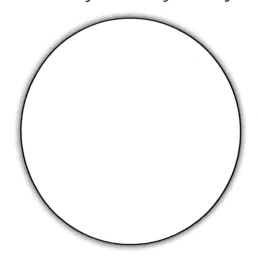

My Progress Today:
The Teeth of My Anger

1 Colour the shark to show how you are feeling: very angry, quite angry or a little angry.

2 By the end of the session were you feeling:

   A bit more angry than usual?

   A bit less angry than usual?

   Just the same?

3 How do you think Greatly was feeling during the storm? Scared? Angry? Lost?

Homework

1 Think about storms and how sometimes they can rage inside our heads.

[empty box]

2 What does our body want to do when we have a storm inside?

[empty box]

3 How can we describe how it feels to have a storm inside us, so that other people understand what we are feeling?

[empty box]

If you can, ask someone at home or friends to help you answer the questions.

Bring your thoughts to the next session and draw a picture if you wish.

[empty box]

Session 7   Integration & Ending

Bringing it all together

Preparation & Resources: Posters and stories from previous sessions; certificates to be presented at the end.

Aim: To integrate the previous sessions and evaluate progress.

Focus: Discussion of previous session and share homework themes.

Warm-Up: Invite group members to lead warm-ups from previous sessions or variations on them.

Main Activities: Introduce the idea that some sessions have focussed on physical movement and games, some on art activities, and others on sculpting and role play:

- Invite participants to choose three contrasting activities from previous sessions to repeat;

- Discuss which activities have assisted them with exploring and understanding their anger.

More Advanced: In pairs, ask group members to create a variation on an exercise from a previous session and take it in turns to lead the group.

Feedback & Sharing: What things have been most useful in exploring angry feelings.

Closure: Read the story of 'How Coyote led the Animals', write Diary Notes, and complete My Progress Today.

Continue with the Story Sheet and WolfWork and then present certificates, and check folders are complete to take home.

The Story

How Coyote Led the Animals

Long ago, a Native American tribe were cold and miserable, they had no fire and two old hags kept it hidden away from humans. Coyote decided to help them, he loved a chance to outwit others, that is in the nature of a trickster.

Coyote went to visit the hags and slowly crept up to their tepee, "It's bitterly cold out here," he said in a pleading voice, "Will you let me come and get warm by your fire?" "He is only a coyote," the witches said to themselves, so called out "Come in and get warm."

Coyote crept in and lay down by the fire, "It is so warm," he thought as he looked around, "I wonder if these hags ever sleep?" He left the next morning having thanked them.

Coyote called a Great Meeting of all the animals to discuss his plan. They came from far away to the land of the Native American tribe. He put them in order from the most strong to the least strong: Lion, Grizzly Bear, Brown Bear, Grey Wolf, Squirrel, and finally Frog.

Coyote went again to the hags' tepee taking an Indian warrior with him who hid behind a hill. He called out "It is bitterly cold, would you let me sit by your fire?"

Again the hags said, "He is only a coyote," and all night he kept watch out of the corner of his eye and tried to plan a way of stealing the fire, and he thought and thought. The next day he went to speak with the Indian and explained his plan. That night, as he settled in the tepee again, the Indian tried to rush inside and the two old hags chased him away. Coyote seized a fire stick and rushed outside. He gave the fire to Lion who started running and gave it to Grizzly Bear who ran some more and gave it to Brown Bear; Brown Bear took the fire and went to Wolf, and Wolf took it to Red Squirrel who set her tail alight and forever has a burn mark on her shoulder – you can see it to this very day. Red Squirrel took the fire to Frog who swallowed it. Frog could not run so he jumped and hopped, but the hags caught up, and grabbed him by the tail. His tail came away in their hands, which is why Frogs have no tails to this day.

Frog kept the fire hidden inside himself and swam under water until he had truly escaped. He surfaced and spat the fire into a pile of dry brushwood and there it rests to this very day. There is always fire inside dry wood and to make it come out, the Indians rub two sticks together.

Story Worksheet

1 How must it feel to have no fire if you live in a cold country?

2 Why did coyote wonder if the old hags ever slept?

3 Think about all the animals that he gathered together, which one do you like most? What qualities does that animal have?

4 Which of the animals would have most difficulty working together?

5 Have you ever noticed that red squirrels have a black mark on their shoulders and that frogs have no tails?

6 Think about this story as a way of using energy to work together rather than being angry with each other: write or draw your thoughts.

WolfWork 7

1 Wolf-cub has achieved something each week in the group. Draw or write on each step of the ladder what you think you have achieved during all the sessions.

2 Draw a picture in the circle of how wolf-cub is feeling now.

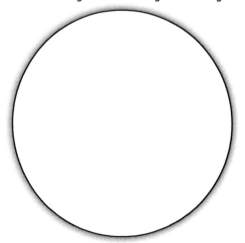

My Progress at the end of the course

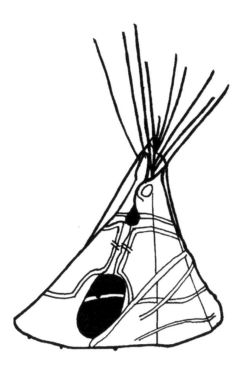

1 Colour the tepee to show if you were feeling lots of anger, some anger or a little anger today.

2 By the end of the session were you feeling:

 A bit more angry than usual?

 A bit less angry than usual?

 Just the same?

3 How do you think Coyote felt when the hags said "He is only a coyote"?

Homework

1 How do you feel now you are at the end of the programme?

2 What advice might you give others who might be feeling angry?

3 Write about what most helped you during the course and draw a calm picture which you could look at if you need it to help you in the future.

(If you can, ask someone at home or friends to help you answer the questions.)

Part 2

Older Children Aged 9–13 Years

Session 1 General Introduction

What do I understand about my anger?

Preparation & Resources: Copies of worksheets from Appendix 2 (Angry Words, Worksheet 3; Diary Notes, Worksheet 4; Rap Poem, Worksheet 5); circle of chairs; soft football; large whiteboard, markers, tambour, and folder for each person.

Aim: To introduce the group to each other, the aims and ground rules of the group.

Focus: Anger issues that affect people now and reflecting on different types of anger.

Warm-Up: Welcome everyone to the circle, and share names; take turns to throw a soft ball and say a person's name; then ask everyone to stand and repeat the name game in a standing circle. Suggest a stop-start run round the room – one tambour beat for stop, 2 beats for run again.

Main Activities: to establish the group and its aims.

- Explain to the group that members have been selected to attend in order to address issues of anger management.

- Invite members to share their own anger issues and different types of anger (refer to the Angry Words Worksheet 3).

- Encourage members to set personal goals for themselves using the Personal Goals Worksheet (p. 60).

- Creating the Ground Rules: Invite group members to contribute ground rules that they feel are important and write them on the white board; contribute essential rules yourself, such as staying in the room, no physical or verbal abuse. (See sample rules, Worksheet 1, Appendix 2).

More Advanced: Explain to the group that the homework consists of themes for them to think about or explore through drawing, encourage them to share ideas in the group now about who they would share with.

Feedback & Sharing: Give everyone a folder or ring binder to hold their worksheets, and invite any questions and discussion.

Closure: Read the Teenage Rap 'Don't Talk to Me' and invite discussion and then complete My Progress Today, and write Diary Notes.

Continue to the Story and Drama Worksheet and the WolfWork.

Teenage Rap: 'Don't Talk To Me'

Don't touch me

Don't talk to me

I don't need your empathy

Just leave me alone

Just let me be angry

You don't know what it's like to be me

You don't know the red mist I see

You don't know the clenched fist when your head's a mess

You don't know what to do when there are no words left

My mouth can't speak

But my body roars

It's a weapon of mass destruction

It's a raging inner war

from the **Actionwork Project**

Story Worksheet

1 How old do you think the person was who wrote this Rap? Was it a boy or girl?

2 Why you think the writer was feeling so angry?

3 Think of the words that you would put into a rap if you were writing your own.

4 Write down a few lines of your own rap and decorate it if you wish.

Drama Worksheet

Warm-Ups & Drama Games

1 Encourage everyone to read the Rap together, starting quietly and getting louder.

2 Divide the group in half and ask the two groups to chant alternate lines.

3 Suggest they add movements to the poem so everyone is moving and chanting together.

Exploration of the Rap

1 In pairs, invite everyone to think about the person who wrote the rap and what might have prompted it.

2 Create a scene between the writer and another person who has made them mad, which shows what might have acted as the trigger.

3 Share the scenes with the whole group and follow up with any questions or discussion.

Personal Goals & Aims

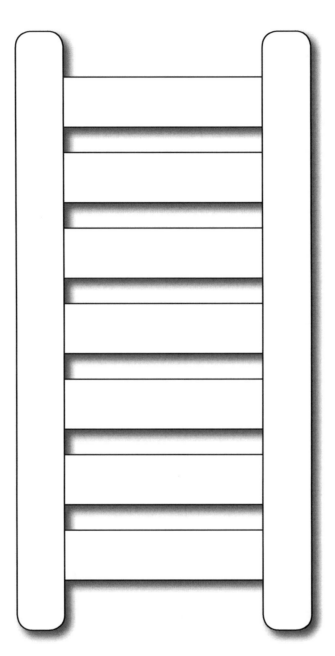

1 At the top of the ladder write your personal goal that you hope to achieve by the end of the seven group sessions.

2 Write on the bottom rung what you think you have achieved in the first session.

3 Write below what you think the most difficult task will be during the course.

 **WolfWork 8**

Draw pictures in the circles and tick the right words in the boxes.

1 Young Wolf is feeling angry
because he or she is scared.
Draw a picture of scared wolf.

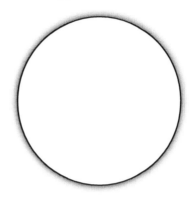

2 Young Wolf feels scared at:

Home ☐ School ☐ Sports ☐ Somewhere else ☐

Write where it is if you wish _____

3 Young Wolf feels scared because of:

Having no brothers or sisters ☐ Being new at the school ☐

Feeling very shy ☐ Something else ☐

Write what this could be _____

4 Young Wolf finds a way to:

Talk to a new friend ☐ Take care of someone ☐

Hold something special ☐ Something else ☐

Write what this could be _____

5 Draw a picture of Young Wolf
caring for another wolf.

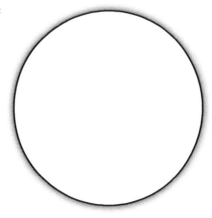

My Personal Progress

Today is the first session of the Anger Management Programme; look at the following questions and see how you think it is going. There is no right answer; it is how you are feeling right now! You can write or draw your answers.

PART 2: SESSION 1
General Introduction

1 Right now I am feeling

More angry than usual ☐

Just the same ☐

Less angry than usual ☐

2 Right now I think the course can be

Very helpful ☐

A bit helpful ☐

Not helpful at all ☐

3 On this course, what would make you feel proud of yourself?

Homework

1 Think about the goal you have set yourself on the Personal Aims worksheet and if possible ask friends or family to support you in what you are doing.

2 Ask other people to say when they feel you have changed your behaviour, even if it is a small step.

3 Think about other angry people in your life who it is easy to copy without realising.

4 If you prefer to draw a picture, draw someone copying another person being angry, and bring your thoughts and pictures to the next session.

Bring any thoughts to the group next time.

Session 2   Anger Out of Control!

My anger is exploding!

Preparation & Resources: Posters of active volcanoes, tambour, folders, plain paper, coloured markers.

Aim: To express and set limits on angry behaviour.

Focus: Discussion of different types of anger.

Warm-Up: Everyone finds a space in the room, when they hear the tambour beat they must shrink as small as possible, then become as large as possible, then jump as high as possible; repeat the exercise with everyone making small sounds, then loud sounds and increasing sounds.

Main Activities: Ask everyone to look at the volcano picture and think about how it moves and what sounds it makes; repeat the following sequence with stop-start on the tambour.

- Everyone moves just their arms as if exploding.

- Everyone moves their arms and makes a volcano sound.

- Everyone finds a space in the room and explodes with their whole body, and makes the sound.

More Advanced: In pairs, body sculpt (see notes in Appendix 3) a volcano and its sound together.

Feedback & Sharing: Talk about where in the body people feel their anger. For some it is in the stomach, for others it is their chest.

Closure: Read the 'Volcano Girl' story, write Diary Notes, and complete My Progress Today.

Continue to Story and Drama Worksheets, and the WolfWork.

The Story

The Volcano Girl

Vinti was a girl who loved everything to do with fire. She would watch her mother light the gas cooker in the kitchen, and as she lit a candle on the table before they ate, and she especially loved it when there was a log fire in the winter and she could watch the flames dancing. Vinti would stare at the bright red embers and see shapes and patterns, and watch the wisps of smoke curling around the wood; she listened to the crackling of the twigs burning and smelled the lovely wood smoke.

Her mother said she was too young to light a fire herself but Vinti thought that at ten she was quite old enough. She had seen the Gipsy children in the camp near the common, and they lit fires themselves and sometimes cooked things on a spike or in a black pot.

In the garden one day when she thought no-one was looking, Vinti gathered some small pieces of wood she found by the bushes, and some logs from the wood shed. She criss-crossed them as she had seen her father do, "It lets the air in," he always said to her as she watched.

But when she lit her fire with matches she had taken from the kitchen, it started to give off horrible smoke that smelt really nasty; it curled its way into the neighbours' gardens and stung her eyes. She was puzzled – it wasn't supposed to be like this! She quickly got some water from the water tank and put out the fire, but that made even more smoke. Eventually it stopped, and Vinti heaved a sigh of relief; but she did not realise that her mother was looking through the bedroom window and had seen what happened …

Story Worksheet

1 What had Vinti seen her mother do with fire?

2 The story says she loved to see the fire dancing, what else did she like about the log fire?

3 Where had she seen children lighting fires?

4 How did her father explain the way he stacked the wood for the fire?

5 What was Vinti feeling when the fire gave off smoke?

6 How do you think the story ends?

 **WolfWork 9**

Draw pictures in the circles and tick the right words in the boxes.

1 Young Wolf is feeling very angry today. Draw a picture of an angry wolf.

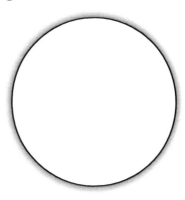

2 Young Wolf's stomach is feeling:

Sick ☐   Fiery ☐   Thumpy ☐   Something else ☐

Write what this could be _____

3 Young Wolf wants to:

Hit someone ☐   Run away ☐

Hide ☐   Do something else ☐

Write what this could be _____

4 What should Young Wolf do to help?

Play football or another sport ☐   Talk to a friend ☐

Tell a teacher ☐   Do something else ☐

Write what this could be _____

5 Draw a picture of Young Wolf feeling calmer.

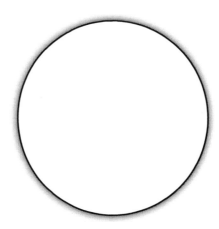

My Progress Today: My Anger Erupts

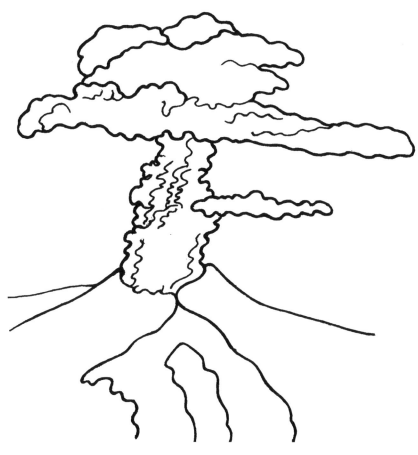

1 Colour the volcano to show whether you were feeling lots of anger, some anger or only a little anger today.

2 By the end of the session were you feeling:

☐ A bit more angry than usual?

☐ A bit less angry than usual?

☐ Just the same?

3 Do you enjoy watching fire? What does it make you feel?

Homework

Things to think about ...

Next time you feel angry notice what your body does:

1 Does your heart beat faster? Are your hands sweaty? Does your stomach thump?

2 Where else in your body do you feel angry? In your stomach? Chest? Somewhere else?

Discuss this with family or a friend if possible, and bring your thoughts to the next session. If you prefer to draw, create an angry picture with your own ideas, or write down any words that make you think of anger.

Session 3   Anger & Nervousness

I am angry because I feel nervous

Preparation & Resources: Lots of hats, caps and scarves, folders, pens and crayons.

Aim: To understand triggers for anger, and what makes people nervous.

Focus: Share thoughts and pictures from homework tasks.

Warm-Up: Invite everyone to choose a hat, cap or scarf and walk around the room as if they are a different person, showing different gestures and facial expressions. After 3 minutes, change hats; repeat several times with no talking, only non-verbal communication is allowed.

Main Activities: Experimenting with different characters and developing confident communication skills. Invite members of the group to:

- Choose a hat, cap or scarf, then walk round the room and show how the character could communicate non-verbally if they were angry.

- Choose another prop and repeat.

- Choose one prop to explore further, and begin to make the sounds of anger.

- Now express the angry words your character might use.

More Advanced: In pairs, *with a basic rule of no touching*, the two characters should talk about what makes them nervous and possibly angry.

Feedback & Sharing: Make sure everyone is out of their character and has removed their hat, cap or scarf. Discuss how it felt to 'act' the anger. What did people learn from their characters?

Closure: Read and discuss 'Sam's Story', write Diary Notes and complete My Progress Today.

Continue to the Story Worksheet and Puppet Drama.

The Story

Sam's Story

Sam gets very nervous, especially when he meets new people. He tries to cover up his nervousness by being angry and rude.

One day, there was a queue of people when he was waiting for the school bus and he pushed his way to the front, just shaking the other people who tried to stop him. The bus was very crowded and there was a lot of pushing and shoving and it was full of people being bad tempered.

He arrived at school late, and to make things worse, there was a new teacher who picked on him because he was late for class. The secretary knew that the bus was late and had explained to the teacher, but Sam just felt he was being picked on. He was far too nervous to say anything to the teacher and the teacher shouted that he was being difficult, and to give him an explanation, please!

Sam retreated into his shell but underneath was simmering, "Why won't somebody just understand how I feel?", he said to himself. When he went quiet he got very stressed which made him feel unwell, with a head and stomach-ache. He wanted to be in a good space, but at the moment he just felt locked in a vicious circle he couldn't escape.

Story Worksheet

1 Why do you think Sam gets nervous?

2 What could help Sam to feel less nervous?

3 Who might be able to help Sam to feel less nervous?

Drama & Puppet Work

1. (Selection of hand/sleeve puppets: wolf, fox, snake, rat, seal, lamb, kitten, giraffe, for example)

  1 Choose a puppet and explore its characteristics and how it communicates.

  2 Work in pairs with two contrasting puppets: one that can be angry and one that can be shy or scared.

  3 Present a short scene with the two puppets to others in the group.

2. If puppets are not appropriate or available for the group, use the following exercises and then the scenes below.

  1 Walk around the room in different moods: a quiet walk, a strong march, a rushing-to-somewhere walk, a worried walk that says "I am late", an angry stomping walk, a slow and thoughtful walk.

  2 Half the group observe the rest walking and call out their guesses of the walking moods – see if they have observed correctly.

  3 In pairs, one person closes their eyes, their partner puts a hand on their shoulder and walks with different paces and moods, and their 'blind' partner has to sense how they are moving and copy how they walk. Vary this with the 'blind' partner changing paces and moods, and the seeing partner having to adapt.

Exploration

a In groups of three, create the scenes of Sam's journey to school but without using any words, only angry gestures.

b Create the scene again but this time adding words.

c Come up with an alternative scene where Sam does not get angry.

d Share the scenes with the other groups and discuss the differences between them.

e Discuss in the group the sorts of tactics which could be helpful in avoiding angry scenes.

WolfWork 10

Draw pictures in the circles and tick the right words in the boxes.

1 Young Wolf feels different and that leads to anger.
Draw a picture of Young Wolf feeling different or strange.

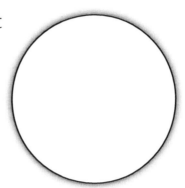

2 How does Young Wolf feel different?

Frightened ☐ Sick ☐ Worried ☐ Something else ☐

Write what this could be _____

3 Young Wolf wants to:

Hurt someone ☐ Hurt himself/herself ☐

Talk to someone ☐ Something else ☐

Write what this could be _____

4 What should Young Wolf do?

Phone a friend ☐ Learn how to juggle ☐

Tell someone at home ☐ Something else ☐

Write what this could be _____

5 Draw a picture of two young wolves.

My Progress Today

Choosing the box that matches the best, draw and colour the hats that you wore in this session:

1 I felt very angry wearing this hat.

2 I felt quite angry wearing this hat.

3 I felt a little angry wearing this hat.

4 I did not feel angry wearing this hat.

What situations make people feel nervous? Write about or draw a situation that would make people feel nervous. Write down three things that we can observe that show someone is feeling anxious or nervous, for instance, biting their finger-nails.

Homework

Things to observe and think about:

1 Watch the different ways that people get angry and what seems to trigger this.

```



```

2 Why do people get anxious or nervous?

```



```

3 What could you say to another person who is anxious or nervous?

```



```

Discuss these questions with family or friends if possible.

Write a description, or if you prefer draw a portrait of a nervous person.

```



```

Session 4   Anger & Bullying

I am angry because I am bullied

Preparation & Resources: Lots of old paperback books (these can be found at charity shops), heavy duty felt-tip pens, scissors/blades, glue-sticks, folders.

Aim: To find ways to use 'journals' to deal with feelings, and improve self-esteem.

Focus: Share thoughts and pictures from homework tasks.

Warm-Up: Invite everyone to walk round the room, first as bullies and then as someone who is bullied, and ask the group to be aware of how their bodies change in the two roles.

Main Activities: Create a personal journal from an old paperback book by decorating it and inserting pictures and statements. Invite everyone in the group to:

- Choose a paperback book for their journal and, using the felt-tip pens, write and decorate their name inside the first pages;

- Choose a page further in and write in heavy felt-tip how you might feel if you were bullied;

- Write on a separate piece of paper: 'Make a loud noise', 'Tell an adult', 'Stay near friends'; tear out two pages from the book and stick this page in their place;

- Write about or draw a picture of a bully, and some words that could be used to describe them.

More Advanced: In pairs, *with a basic rule of no laughing*, talk about what it feels like to be bullied.

Feedback & Sharing: Discuss journals and how they can be used to record feelings and also ways of dealing with anger – not just bullying.

Closure: Read and discuss Vinti's story, write Diary Notes and complete My Progress Today.

Move onto the Story and Drama Worksheets and WolfWork.

The Story

Vinti with the unusual name

When everyone returned to school after the holidays, they discovered that they had a new teacher. He called out the register and looked at each person as they put up their hand, "Vinti Meyer? That's an unusual name" he said, and smiled. Vinti smiled back. Then she blushed when she heard someone sniggering and other people whispering. A boy sitting behind her copied the teacher and said "Vinti. What an unusual name!" and giggled to himself. Vinti felt awful, her heart was beating faster and she knew she was blushing.

At play time, a group of children started chanting, "Vinti, Minti, what an UNUSUAL name", and then screamed with laughter. Her two best friends said to her, " Just ignore them, they will soon get bored". But they didn't and they followed Vinti around the playground. Her face was burning and her stomach churned and inside she wanted to scream but nothing would come out.

What could she do?

Story Worksheet

1 Why do you think the teacher commented on Vinti's name?

2 How do you think Vinti was feeling inside?

3 Give another example of something that might make children whisper and laugh.

4 Do you think that sometimes children stop doing things in case they are laughed at?

Drama Worksheet

Warm-Ups & Drama Games

1 In the circle, one person starts by turning to the person on their left and making a simple movement, that person copies the movement exactly, and then repeats it to the person on their own left; the next person does the same; they repeat the movement to the giver, and then repeat it to the person on their left. This continues all the round the group. See if the movement can stay the same until the end of the circle.

2 In pairs, imagine one person is a dog and the other person is holding their lead, move around the room with the dog owner in charge, directing or pulling the dog this way and that. Then swap so the dog is in charge and the owner has to follow.

3 Repeat with one person being a jockey holding a horse's reins and the other is a runaway horse, change over.

4 Practice the game so it looks real even though there is no lead or rein.

(If appropriate, the puppets can be used to explore the bully and the bullied person, see previous exercise.)

Exploration

In groups of five:

a Discuss and create the scene where the children are whispering behind her back, taking it in turns to be Vinti.

b Discuss and create the scene where Vinti is getting bullied in the playground (take it in turns to play Vinti).

c Experiment with different ways that Vinti could respond (remember the three things that were written in the journal: 'Make a loud noise', 'Tell an adult', 'Stay near friends') and see if they work.

d Closure: Share the dramas and discuss how this situation could be changed. Suggest that everyone draws a picture or writes something in their diary notes.

WolfWork 11

Draw pictures in the circles and tick the right words in the boxes.

1 Young Wolf is feeling angry because of being teased. Draw a picture in the circle of how Young Wolf is feeling right now:

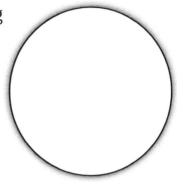

2 Young Wolf is being teased by:

One child ☐   Group of children ☐

Brother or sister ☐   Someone else ☐

Write who it is if you wish _____

3 Young Wolf is being teased because of:

Different looks ☐   A different way of talking ☐

Being very shy ☐   Something else ☐

Write what it is if you wish _____

4 Young Wolf finds a way to:

Tell the bully to stop ☐   Ask a friend to help ☐

Tell a teacher ☐   Something else ☐

Write what it is if you wish

_____

5 Draw a picture of a young wolf being playful.

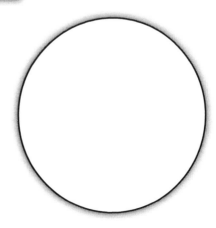

My Progress Today

1 I felt very angry when I was playing the part of:

Teacher ☐   Vinti ☐   Bully ☐

Another child ☐

2 I felt very unhappy when I was playing the part of:

Teacher ☐   Vinti ☐   Bully ☐

Another child ☐

3 I think Vinti's teacher should:

☐   Punish the bully

☐   Be careful what he says to children

☐   Talk to the whole class

☐   Talk to Vinti and cheer her up

4 Draw a picture, or write about Vinti being bulled.

Homework

Things to think about ...

1 Next time you see someone being bullied think about how you would feel.

2 What would you do if you were bullied?

3 What might people bully you about?

(Discuss these questions with family and friends if you can.)

Bring your thoughts to the next session. Draw a portrait or write a description of a bully.

Session 5   Anger & Confusion

I am angry because I am confused

Preparation & Resources: Pictures of meerkats, folders, white board, coloured markers, blank paper. Materials for puppet-making (p. 90).

Aim: To provide opportunities for participants to be heard and seen, and to begin to sort out confusions.

Focus: Discussion of different types of anger, different reasons for it, write reasons for angry feelings on the board.

Warm-Up: Physical stretch and run round the room; stop and freeze as if: whispering, then calling, then shouting, then screaming (all with no sound).

Main Activities: Working with a partner, choose young own calling sound:

- One person closes their eyes and has to find their partner who is somewhere in the room, making the sound (but of course lots of other sounds are being called!);

- Change over with a new sound if preferred;

- With the same partner, one person listens while the other completes the sentence 'What I really want to tell you is …'

- Change over and repeat.

More Advanced: Elaborate the sentence completion: the first time the questionner has their back turned and the second time they are facing the listener.

Feedback & Sharing: How can people be listened to when we don't understand? Especially without being angry?

Closure: Read the story: 'The Meerkat who Faded Away', complete My Progress Today, and write Diary Notes.

Continue with the Story and Puppet Drama sheets, and WolfWork.

The Story

The Meerkat who Faded Away

The Meerkat group who lived in the south desert was growing very rapidly; there seemed to be more and more families moving in and burrowing their own holes, and there were more and more Meerkats to protect and feed. One group had only a few adults but lots of young ones, so many that it seemed they were always counting each other to make sure they were all there.

Millie was the middle Meerkat in a family of seven children: she was number four and did not like it at all. The older ones said she was too young to play with them, and the little ones were far too babyish for her. Mum and Dad were too busy to take notice of the youngsters squabbling. Millie became more and more confused and withdrawn, and whenever she tried to talk to her Mum, she would just say "Not now, I am busy". She hated being told to 'run-along' or 'find something to do' or 'stop being so demanding'.

Millie began to sit on her own and she stopped eating with the others, but no-one noticed, and as she did not eat and got thinner and thinner, her coat began to lose its gloss and her eyes became very cloudy. "Nobody cares," she said to herself as another ignoring day passed by, and she felt unhappy. However, someone did notice her. It was the old grandmother from another Meerkat group who was too old to be very active, but each day she would walk and sit, and look around.

One morning Grandmother was waiting when Millie came out to find a hiding place and said to her, "Well young Millie, I wonder if you could give me a hand?" Millie was so startled that someone had spoken to her that she jumped! "Sorry, can you say that again … please?" "I was hoping you could give me a hand as I go for my walk, I find it very difficult." Millie was very surprised to be asked to help, and willingly helped the old Meerkat along. "Time to rest for a moment," said Grandmother as they came to a bush that offered a little shade. It really was very, very hot. They sat together and Millie began to talk, and she talked and talked as if she would never stop. Here at last was someone who did not ignore her. Maybe her life could change.

Story Worksheet

(Write or draw your answers)

1 What happened to Millie that she became so neglected?

2 Why was she so confused?

3 What made her stop eating?

4 What could she have done earlier to stop this happening?

5 Who did Millie need to listen to her?

6 What will happen to Millie now?

Puppet Drama Worksheet

Making a Puppet

Materials needed: old newspapers, masking tape, large coloured markers, wood glue, sticks such as a dowel rods.

Suggest everyone creates their own meerkat puppet; they can choose which character in the story they wish to make.

Scrunch up pieces of newspaper to make a head, and cover with masking tape, press it to give it shape and features; draw facial expressions with heavy felt pens; attach a stick using wood glue.

Once the wood glue is dry, create the story in small groups of what happened to Millie and make up a new ending.

OR

Acquire meerkat sleeve puppets and group members can make the expressions by moving the puppets' mouths.

If the group is unready for puppet work, suggest that everyone draw a picture of a meerkat who is confused and shares a story about their character.

WolfWork 12

Draw pictures in the circles and tick the right words in the boxes.

1 Young Wolf is feeling angry because he or she is muddled or confused. Draw a picture of a confused wolf.

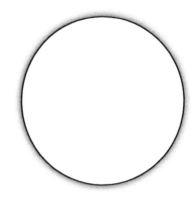

2 Young Wolf is feeling muddled about:

Home ☐   School ☐   Friends ☐   Something else ☐

Write what it is if you wish _____

3 Young Wolf is feeling angry because:

Grown-ups don't answer questions ☐

Teachers are too busy to talk ☐   Children don't listen ☐

Another reason ☐

Write what it is if you wish _____

4 Young Wolf finds a way to:

Insist on time with an adult (perhaps ask in a note) ☐

Explain to a teacher (classroom assistant could help) ☐

Draw a picture of how they are feeling ☐

Something else ☐

Write what it is if you wish

_____

5 Draw a picture of a young wolf talking with another wolf.

My Progress Today:
My Anger Started Sadly

1 Colour the Meerkat to show how you were feeling: lots of anger, some anger or a little anger today.

2 By the end of the session were you feeling:

 A bit more angry than usual?

 A bit less angry than usual?

 Just the same?

3 What advice would you give to Millie to stop her becoming so unhappy?

Homework

1 Think about who you would like to talk to most and what you need to sort out.

2 How can you get that person's attention without being angry or making them angry?

3 Is there anyone who can help you speak to this person?

(If you can, ask someone at home or friends to help you answer the questions.)

Bring your thoughts to the next session and write some notes or draw a picture if you prefer.

Session 6 Anger & Rejection

Anger at being abandoned

Preparation & Resources: Cloaks, wraps, walking sticks and caps, as props for drama work.

Aim: To explore the theme and outcome of the story, and any resonances it may have for group members.

Focus: Share homework thoughts and pictures, remind group members that there are many feelings which can make us angry, including fear and rejection.

Warm-Up: Invite the group to make as much noise as possible by stamping their feet, clapping their hands, and experiment with beating their chests, slapping their legs and so on (body percussion); in groups of three, two people hold hands and the third person tries to enter the circle: ground rules of no tickling and no flying tackles! The secret is to get in by stealth. Changeover so everyone has a chance to 'break-in'. Also try breaking out of the circle using the same principles.

Main Activities: Invite everyone to share any famous stories they know about people being abandoned: Moses in the Bullrushes (there are several in Shakespeare and from ancient Greece); there are ancient tales on TV and in films, as well as more modern ones on programmes such as soaps, police dramas and so on.

- Where might babies be abandoned? (church doorways, hospitals) Why might babies be abandoned? (illness, mother not coping)

- When are children fostered or adopted? (parents can't cope, parents can't keep children safe)

- Who is involved in adoption and fostering? (police, social workers)

- Read the story of 'Zal the White-Haired Baby' and invite feedback.

More advanced: In pairs, ask people to create a story about an abandoned child and then share it without using words.

Feedback & Sharing: Suggest that everyone thinks about how it must feel to be abandoned.

Closure: Read the story of Zal again, then complete My Progress Today, write Diary Notes and My Personal Journal.

Continue onto the Story and Drama Worksheets, then WolfWork.

The Story

Zal the White-Haired Baby

In ancient times a great warrior gave birth to a baby boy with pure white hair. The baby was very beautiful but his father was scared that he was a demon. He decided to abandon the baby on a hill side, and so with great sorrow he journeyed to a far-away mountain and left the baby there.

The child was found by a shepherd and his wife, and was cared for as if he was their own. They had no children and were glad to adopt this abandoned baby who they named 'Zal'. They did not notice his white hair in their delight at having a child at last. He grew up to be strong and powerful and became a great warrior like his father.

Zal's father always felt great sadness that he had abandoned his child and many years later, decided to go and search for him. Was he still alive after all these years? Had he died from exposure on the mountain as a tiny child?

He walked for many days to the far-away mountain and asked many people if they knew of a child being found all those years ago. Eventually, a shepherd family said that their uncle and aunt had found a baby and brought him up. The baby was now a young man and very proud and strong. They told the father where to find the shepherd's house.

He went to the village and found the house. There was a young man with pure white hair coming out of the door. The warrior knew that this must be his son. He approached him and said …

Story Worksheet

1 How do you think Zal felt as he was growing up not knowing his birth-parents?

2 Did his parents regret that they had abandoned him?

3 Why do you think it was such a long time before his father went to find him?

4 If you like, draw a picture of Zal in his warrior clothes, looking proud and strong.

Drama Worksheet

Warm-Ups & Drama Games

1 Play a chase game, one person is 'It', and when another person is caught they join up by holding hands; continue until the whole group is caught and joined together.

2 Imagine there is a large circle in the centre of the room (draw it with chalk if possible); ask people to walk across the room from corner to corner, and when they enter the circle something happens to them: sticking to the floor, electric currents, freezing cold, blown by winds and so on.

3 Try the same exercise with two people together and reacting to the same stimulus; maybe one can help the other to get out of the circle.

Exploration through the drama

a Create the scene where the baby is found by the shepherd (use some rolled-up cloth for the baby – dolls never look real enough!)

b What discussion might take place between the birth mother and father after they have abandoned the child?

c Create your own ending for the story, what actually happened after the birth father was sure he had seen his son?

Share the scenes and discuss the different endings.

Closure: write in your Personal Journal or draw a picture about today's story.

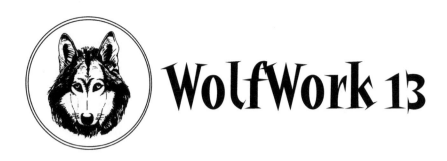

WolfWork 13

Draw pictures in the circles and tick the right words in the boxes.

1 Young Wolf is feeling angry because he or she feels rejected or ignored. Draw a picture of a wolf feeling rejected.

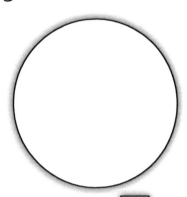

2 Young Wolf is feeling ignored at:

Home ☐   School ☐   After school or Saturday club ☐

Somewhere else ☐

Write where it is if you wish _____

3 Young Wolf is feeling rejected because:

Grown ups are never there ☐   Teachers don't listen ☐

Children laugh or walk away ☐   Another reason ☐

Write what it is if you wish _____

4 Young Wolf finds a way to:

Find another adult who will listen ☐

Speak to someone at after-school club ☐

Be friendly with someone who has just moved in ☐

Something else ☐

Write what it is if you wish

_____

5 Draw a picture of a young wolf 'high-fiving' with another wolf.

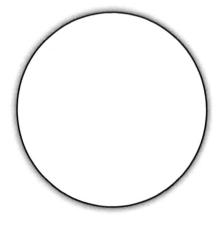

My Progress Today

1 Today I feel I can understand my angry feelings better. Colour in the circle to show your level of understanding.

○ I can understand my feelings a lot.

○ I can understand my feelings a bit.

○ I can understand my feelings a little.

2 Draw a rose bush and colour it in to how you are feeling.

3 Draw a picture of a baby that has been left on a hillside. Do you think there was a message left with the baby?

Homework

Things to think about …

1 Do the new parents tell their child that they were abandoned?

> (blank answer box)

2 What story should the new parents tell the child when they are old enough?

> (blank answer box)

3 Think of the letter that the birth parents might write for the baby to read when it is older.

> (blank answer box)

(Discuss with family and friends if possible.)

If you prefer to draw a picture, draw the baby being found by someone who really wants a baby, or describe how this might feel.

> (blank answer box)

Session 7   Anger & Resolution

Integrating all the sessions

Preparation & Resources: Make sure all the resources that have been used during the seven sessions are available including the circle of chairs.

Aim: To bring together the several themes of the programme and to look at people's progress throughout.

Focus: Invite everyone to bring thoughts and feelings from the previous session and share any pictures they have drawn.

Warm-Up: Suggest that everyone starts off in the circle and talks about their 'journey through the course'. Place sheets of newspaper at intervals around the room and suggest to the group that these are stepping stones and they have to go from step to step as if it was their journey on the course, without slipping or tearing the paper.

Main Activities: Invite everyone to look through their folders and Personal Journals and share with the group the most difficult things they have done.

- Share difficult exercises and whether people feel they have achieved them.

- Share difficult changes people have made and how group members feel about the changes.

- Invite group members to comment on other people's changes as well.

- Celebrate everyone's sense of achievement with what they have accomplished.

More Advanced: Suggest that people can tell the group the hopes and fears they had when they joined the group.

Feedback & Sharing: Ask the group what they would change if the course was to run again. Would they could recommend the group to others?

Closure: Read the story of 'St Anthony and his Pig', write or draw a closing entry in Diary Notes, continue to the Story and Drama Worksheets and WolfWork, write My Personal Journal and complete My Progress Today, present certificates.

The Story

St Anthony & His Pig

Years ago, near the Mediterranean Sea, the land was cold and dark, and the villagers had no fire and could not cook and had to huddle together to keep warm. They were so miserable that they decided to ask St Anthony to help them. He lived alone in the fields and looked after animals. He was curious when some of the villagers came to bring him some vegetables.

The oldest woman said "St Anthony, cravin' your pardon sir – we are all quite desperate – please can you find a way for us to have fire and light?"

Anthony said to them, "Go back to your village and stay quiet together with your eyes closed, and keep a picture of the fire in your minds." The villagers did what he said, and St Anthony decided he must go to hell as that is where all the fire was.

He went with his stick and pet pig, down a steep path and knocked on the gates of hell. "Who are you?" said a small devil, "Go away – we only have sinners here!" Then he saw the pig and thought "Roast pork for dinner!" He opened the door a crack and the pig charged in and caused absolute chaos, knocking over benches and breaking things.

Another young devil called out to Anthony, "Come and get your pig" and Anthony touched the pig with his stick and immediately it became calm. He told the devils that his stick needed to dry out and put it in the fire.

Then he left the gates of hell with his pig at his heels, and returned to the people of the village. They had piled up twigs and branches and he put his stick in the middle and the wood caught alight. The villagers shouted with joy, taking a firebrand to light their own fires; they were finally able to bake bread, and remembered to take some to St Anthony.

Anthony reminded them to take fire to all the other nearby villages, which in turn took it to some more, and soon everyone had fire. And now, during the dark winter months they are able to sit round their fires and tell stories.

 ℗ This page may be photocopied for instructional use only. © *The Anger Management Toolkit*, S. Jennings, 2011

Story Worksheet

1 What might have happened if the devils had managed to separate
St Anthony from his pet pig?

2 There are many stories about the world having no fire; what would it
really be like to have no fire? How would people manage? What would
be the most difficult thing to do with no fire?

3 The story says that St Anthony lived on his own with his pet pig: what
sort of things would he have eaten?

Drama Worksheet

Warm-Ups & Drama Games

1 Invite everyone to imagine they are Anthony climbing down a very steep and stony path that twists and turns, and sometimes the stones are dislodged and people almost slip over.

2 Suggest that people take it in turns to be the pig running around hell with the others being all the little devils chasing but not catching them.

Exploration of the Story

a Ask the group to divide into smaller groups and to imagine they are the villagers: who is it suggests that they should ask Anthony to help them? Who is brave enough to speak for everyone?

b Create the scene in the underworld where the pig is causing mayhem and Anthony is quietly acquiring the fire.

c Point out to the group that Anthony immediately suggests that another village should benefit from the fire as well; invite them to create the scene where half the group stay and prepare a huge feast (do they invite Anthony?) and the other half go and present a brand of fire to the next village.

d Share the scenes with each other.

Alternatively, the story can be explored through puppets that the group make, or character sleeve puppets that can be acquired.

My progress through the course

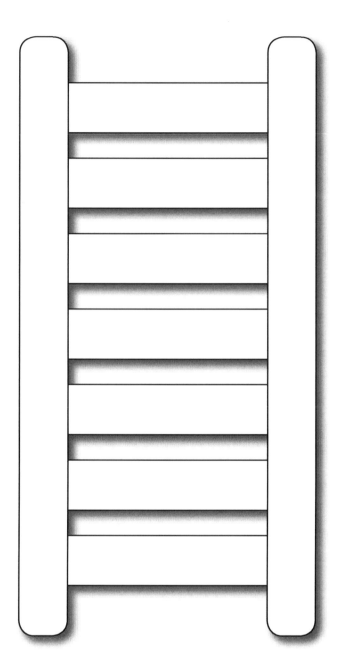

1 Fill in every step of the ladder with something that you have achieved during the seven weeks.

2 Which was the most difficult step to climb to?

3 Did you have any doubts that you would make it?

WolfWork 14

Draw pictures in the circles and tick the right words in the boxes.

1 Young Wolf wants to make things work now; maybe other people understand the anger more than they did. Draw two wolves having some fun.

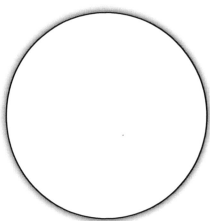

2 Young Wolf has learned that some things can get better by:

Telling a grown-up how you feel ☐

Telling a best friend how you feel ☐

Doing something very different ☐

Something else ☐

Write it down if you wish _____

3 Draw a picture of how you are feeling now you have finished the course.

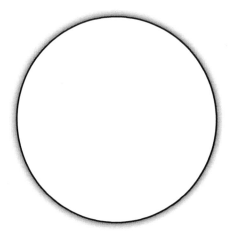

My Progress through The Course

1 Think about and congratulate yourself on your achievements and write them below. Accept the certificate when it is presented to you and be proud of it.

2 Think about when you arrived on the course and write down or draw the difference between then and now.

3 Write down or draw the things that might pull you back to being angry again.

Draw a personal flag for yourself that says: 'I Did It'.

Think about friends and family with whom you can share your success.

Part 3

Teenagers Aged 14–17 years

Session 1   General Introduction

What can I do with my anger?

Preparation & Resources: Large whiteboard, large markers, tambour, and a folder for each person.

Aim: To introduce the group to each other, the aims and ground rules of the group. (Sample rules can be found in Worksheet 1, Appendix 2.)

Focus: Anger issues affective lives of group members now, and reflecting on different types of anger.

Warm-Up: Welcome everyone to the group and encourage members to share their names, and invite questions about the group and its purpose.

Main Activities: To establish the group and its aims.

- Explain to the group members that they have been selected to address issues of anger management.

- Invite members to share their own anger issues and different types of anger (refer to the Angry Words, Worksheet 3, Appendix 2).

- Encourage members to set personal goals for themselves using the Personal Goals Worksheet (p. 117).

- Creating the Ground Rules: Invite group members to contribute ground rules that they feel are important and write them on the white board; contribute essential rules such as staying in the room, no physical or verbal abuse.

More Advanced: Explain to the group that the homework for the course will consist of themes for them to think about or draw, encourage them to suggest ideas now about who they might discuss their thoughts with.

Feedback & Sharing: Give everyone a folder to hold completed worksheets, and invite any questions and discussion; explain that Personal Journals will be created in a later session (5).

Closure: Read the story and end with My Progress Today, or continue with the Story and Drama Worksheets or WolfWork below.

Story

An Angry Situation

Police were called to a house in Neville Road in the early hours of the morning. Neighbours reported loud banging and crashing in the house and shouting and screaming. The police forced their way into the house when no-one answered the door.

Neighbours said that they did not know the people who lived in the house, there were two or three adults who kept themselves to themselves. "They moved in about six months ago," said one neighbour. "They nodded if I said anything, but they didn't have much to say." Another one commented "This is the first time there has been any noise, it started about midnight, woke everyone up, very shocking."

Some shouting continued after the police entered the house, and a second police car arrived, followed by an ambulance.

Neighbours witnessed one person being restrained and taken forcibly from the house into the ambulance, and a second person, in floods of tears, being ushered into a police car by a female police officer. Other police officers took witness statements from neighbours. The police refused to comment, saying only that it was unlikely that they would be pressing criminal charges.

Later, a third adult was seen repairing the front door where it had been broken, and removing broken furniture from the house.

Story Worksheet

(Write or draw your answers)

1 Who do you think was angry with whom in this newspaper report?

2 Why do you think one person was taken away by ambulance?

3 How do you think the three people might be related to each other?

4 How would it have changed the story if the person being restrained had been taken away in the police car?

Drama Worksheet

Warm-Ups & Drama Games

1 Invite everyone to throw the soft ball and call out their names until everyone in the group knows each other's name; if they already know each other, play the game using names they prefer to be called.

2 Using the tambour, play 'stop-start', where people run round the room and stop at one beat and start again at two.

3 Shakey-shake: standing in a circle, ask everyone to lift their right arm and shake it very vigorously, then their left arm, then their right leg, then their left leg, then call out "All together!" and everything has to shake. Repeat to get the energy going and until participants seem more relaxed.

Exploration of the Situation

a Read the story through together and invite comments on who the people were, and why there might have been extreme anger.

b In small groups, create the main scenes in body sculpts and freeze frames (see Appendix 3) of what happened (maximum five frames).

c In pairs, role-play two neighbours discussing what has happened.

d Imagine you are the person mending the door; create a scene where this person is talking to a friend about what happened.

Personal Goals & Aims

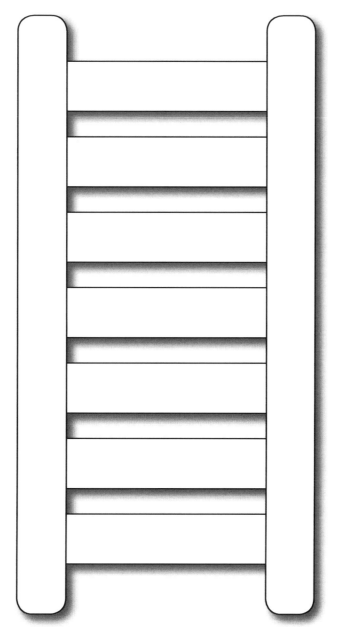

1 At the top of the ladder write your personal goal to achieve by the end of the seven group sessions.

2 Write on the bottom rung what you think you have achieved in the first session.

3 Write below what you think the most difficult task will be during the course.

My Progress Today

At the end of today's session, how are you feeling?
Fill in any circles that apply to you.

I am feeling a lot of anger inside me.

I am feeling some anger inside me.

I enjoyed the physical games in the group.

I enjoyed meeting other people

I am beginning to understand my anger.

What makes you angry most of all? Write your ideas below.

WolfWork 15

Colour the Wolf Picture and then think about the questions below

What do you think these wolves are feeling? _____

_____

Tick the box you feel think describes the feelings.

1 Anger ☐

2 Sadness ☐

3 Fear ☐

Homework

1 Think about why you are coming to this group and what you would like to achieve.

2 Ask other people to tell you when they feel you have changed your behaviour, even if it is a small step.

3 Think about other angry people in your life who it is easy to copy without realising you are doing it.

4 If you prefer to draw a picture, draw someone copying another person being angry, or describe how this might feel.

Bring any thoughts to the group next time. If you prefer, design a large poster of a wolf.

Session 2   Anger that Erupts

My anger is boiling!

Preparation & Resources: Folders, Worksheets from Appendix 2 (3: Angry Words, 6: Anger Thermometer, 9 & 10: Triggers), large whiteboard and markers, coloured pens, circle of chairs, soft football.

Aim: To explore different words and the degree of anger they convey.

Focus: Triggers that can start the angry feelings.

Warm-Up: Invite group members to sit in the circle, remind them of the contract agreed in the first session; check out any questions or clarifications about the group, and share pictures and words from homework. (If people are restless, suggest a physical warm-up with throwing and catching the soft ball before sitting in the circle.)

Main Activities: Using charts to measure degrees of anger; triggers and responses. Ask group members to:

- Fill in the Anger Thermometer chart to show how they are feeling now.

- Look at the Angry Words worksheet and invite people to suggest other words: these can be written on the white board.

- Create a list on the white board of triggers for angry responses: for example 'I get mad when a teacher accuses me unfairly'. Look at the Triggers Worksheets.

More Advanced: Discuss with a partner the most common triggers for your anger.

Feedback & Sharing: Invite group members to share their different levels of anger and their most common triggers.

Closure: Ask the Group to fill in My Progress Today and move onto the Story and Drama work.

The Story

'You Can't Do That!'

Jem slipped into the park just before the gates were due to be locked, and hid in some bushes near the path. He was pretty sure the park-keeper would lock this gate last of all. No-one was around, so quickly he ran out and pulled up some plants: clumps with lots of buds that were beginning to flower, and dark green leaves. He knew his mum would like the flowers now she was home again. Quickly, he shoved them into his jacket pockets, made sure his hoodie was up, and ran towards the gate.

"Hey, you can't do that!" shouted the park-keeper, breaking into a run. Unfortunately for Jem, he stumbled, giving the keeper time to catch up and grab him. "You kids, you just make me mad," yelled the keeper, "always spoiling things", and he landed a strong punch that made Jem lose his balance and sprawl on the grass. "You need a lesson, you all do," said the keeper, giving him a hard kick, followed by another, as Jem doubled up in pain. "Get out before I call the police," he said, standing over Jem and wondering whether to kick him again. Jem tried to roll over to protect himself, but suddenly another kick struck him.

Jem staggered up, in great pain, shoving the park-keeper off balance as he lurched towards the gate and managed to escape, making sure his face was still hidden. He couldn't run very fast as his side was killing him and he felt really sick. A few minutes later he stopped to get his breath, worried that he might have been followed.

Story Worksheet

1 Why is it so important for Jem to get some flowers?

2 What would the 'Anger Thermometer' look like for the park-keeper?

3 What is a likely anger trigger for the park-keeper?

4 What might Jem do next? Has his own anger been triggered?

Drama Worksheet

Warm-Ups & Drama Games

1 Suggest that everyone throws and catches the soft ball as they run round the room.

2 In pairs, one person takes the role of someone who saw the incident with Jem in the park, and the other person is Jem. Jem starts to tell the story of what happened and the witness must interrupt, saying "No, he didn't"; Jem has to change the story and continue; the witness interrupts several times with "No, he didn't" and each time Jem has to change his story. Change round with one person being the park-keeper and the other interrupting.

3 Still working with the same partner, compare how much of the story was changed from what actually happened.

Exploration of the Story

a Encourage group members to focus on the triggers for anger in the story and to create a scene in threes where either the park-keeper is triggered or Jem is triggered after he leaves the park.

b Suggest to group members that Jem arrives home and his mum is very angry – explore what has triggered her anger. That he is untidy and grubby? That he is limping? Another reason? Explore the scene.

c Jem still has the plants in his pockets: create a scene in small groups where he finishes what he wanted to do with the plants.

d Close the drama session with 'de-roling', deep breathing and calm down to music; followed by a discussion of the issues.

WolfWork 16

1 Colour the Wolf Picture and think about the relationship between the two wolves.

1 Are they both feeling angry? ☐

2 Are they playing? ☐

3 Is one wolf more angry than the other? ☐

My Progress Today

1 By the end of the session were you feeling:

☐   A bit more angry than usual?

☐   A bit less angry than usual?

☐   Just the same?

2 What is the most common trigger for your anger?

3 Complete the following sentence: 'When I get angry I want to ...'

4 Draw a picture or describe what you do when you get angry.

Homework

Things to think about …

Notice the triggers that start your angry cycle (look at the Triggers Worksheets again to remind yourself).

Draw symbols or pictures or write down words to remind you of your triggers.

Try to discuss your triggers with family and friends, and ask them if they have noticed any triggers. Bring any thoughts and drawings to the next session.

Session 3   Anger & Anxiety

I am angry because I am anxious

Preparation & Resources: Folders, Worksheets 7 and 8, Worry Scale and Worries and Anxieties, from Appendix 2, large whiteboard and markers, coloured pens, circle of chairs, soft football.

Aim: To look at issues of anxiety.

Focus: Worried feelings.

Warm-Up: Invite group members to sit in a circle, remind them of the group contract; check out any questions or clarifications people may have; and share pictures, symbols and words from homework (Triggers for Anger); physical warm-up: throwing and catching ball or 'start/stop'.

Main Activities: Use the Worksheets to measure degrees of worry and degrees of anxiety. Ask group members to:

- Fill in the 'Worry Scale' to describe how they are feeling now.

- Look at 'My Worries & Anxieties' Worksheet and discuss the ways people feel anxious: staying awake at night, being unable to concentrate, for example.

- Complete the worksheets and place in folders.

More Advanced: Discuss with a partner something that causes you anxiety.

Feedback & Sharing: Invite group members to discuss how expressing anger can be a way of avoiding anxiety.

Closure: Ask everyone to fill in their Personal Progress sheet and move onto the Story and Drama Work.

Story

'What if ...?'

Madeline was used to worrying and she felt she had plenty to worry about.

She lived with her Mum and Dad and younger sister, and her Nan lived two streets away. It took Madeline almost an hour to walk to school in the morning and another hour back home again in the afternoon. Her main worries were that Mum had a mental illness and spent a lot of time in bed, and also her Dad getting angry if meals were not ready on time, and expecting Madeline to sort everything out.

She had to get up early every morning, make breakfasts, wash Mum and make sure her sister was ready for school. She also had to do shopping for her Nan twice a week as well as the family shopping. She felt guilty when she got angry, but she resented the fact that she couldn't go out after school, her mates couldn't come home with her, and her homework suffered because she was so tired.

She was always asking herself: What if Mum got worse? What if Nan had a fall? What if her sister had an accident? What if Dad left them? All her worrying and 'What if?' questions stopped her eating very much and she started to get very thin. Inside, she was very angry and snapped when people asked her questions, or friends showed concerns. She started slapping and pinching her sister – but only when no-one else was looking. Soon everything got too much ...

Story Worksheet

1 Why is Madeline so angry?

2 Who is she angry with?

3 Which of the 'What if?' questions do you think worries Madeline the most?

4 Who could help Madeline with her feelings?

Drama Worksheet

Warm-Ups & Drama Games

1 Invite group members to play tag, but you can only avoid being caught if you stand back-to-back with someone else, for a count of three.

2 Suggest that everyone works in pairs, one person starts by saying "You must" and the other says "I can't" and allows it to develop into a situation; change over and repeat, (explore variations such as "I won't", "You will").

3 Allow the same scenes to be explored by using gestures and no words or sounds.

Exploration of the Story

a Encourage group members to focus on the anxiety that Madeline is experiencing about others; in threes create a scene where a teacher tells her off for not finishing her homework, and another student tries to defend her; is Madeline angry with the teacher? Appreciative of the other student?

b Suggest to group members that Madeline arrives home and her dad is very angry – explore the scene in small groups as to why he is angry.

c Madeline faints one day in class – invite group members to explore in a scene what happens next.

d Discuss in the group what might happen next in Madeline's story, and explore in a scene possible endings to the situation, answering the question, 'Who else might need to be involved?'

e Close the drama session with 'de-roling', deep breathing and calm down to music; followed by discussion.

WolfWork 17

Colour the Wolf Picture and think about the fact that the wolf is on its own.

Write or draw your answers.

1 Why do you think this wolf is on its own?

2 Would it prefer to be with other wolves?

3 Which wolf might be a friend to this one?

My Progress Today

1 By the end of the session were you feeling:

☐ A bit more angry than usual?

☐ A bit less angry than usual?

☐ Just the same?

2 What is the most common event that makes you anxious?

3 Complete the following sentence: 'When I get anxious I want to …'

4 Write a description or draw a picture of what you do when you get anxious.

Homework

Things to think about …

Notice the anxiety habits that you have (e.g., biting nails, sweaty hands).

Draw pictures or write words to remind you of when you feel anxious.

Try to discuss your anxieties with family and friends, and ask them if they have observed any times when you are anxious. Bring any thoughts and pictures to the next meeting.

Session 4   Anger & Intimidation

I am angry because I am intimidated by others

Preparation & Resources: Folders, white board, large coloured pens, Worksheet 11 from Appendix 2 'Why are People Intimidated?'

Aim: To find ways to acknowledge feeling about being intimidated.

Focus: Share thoughts and pictures from homework tasks

Warm-Up: Invite everyone to walk round the room, first as people who intimidate and then as someone being intimidated, and ask the group to be aware how their bodies change between the two roles. Suggest they also interact with a partner using only gestures and other non-verbal communication, taking turns to be intimidator and intimidated.

Main Activities: Invite everyone in the group to:

- Write on the board words to describe feelings that occur when people are intimidated.

- Look at and complete the Worksheet 'Why are People Intimidated?' and discuss thoughts and feelings that arise.

More Advanced: In pairs, with a basic rule of no laughing, talk about what it feels like to be intimidated.

Feedback & Sharing: Discuss feelings noted on Worksheets and put them in folders.

Discuss the situation described in the story, how it could be acted out as a drama, and who would play which part. If the group is ready to move on, explore the Story Worksheet or move onto the Drama exploration and exercises. Otherwise, close the session after the discussion.

Story

'I can't do it again ...'

Freddie was always anxious to please. At home he always helped around the house, especially after his mum had the twins. She was really tired and Freddie would fetch and carry for her and hold one baby while she fed the other one. Sometimes he gave one of the babies a bottle, holding her just like his mum showed him. There was just so much to do. He already had a younger brother, and now there were the twins, both girls, and his dad's sister also lived with them because she used a wheelchair and needed help.

At school the teachers often said how helpful he was; he was 'sensible' they said, and gave him duties like helping with registration, making sure the right books were handed out, and welcoming new pupils to the school as they were usually a bit shy or nervous. He was good at his school work and generally the teachers thought he had 'promise'.

Today was different; he knew it as soon as he walked through the school gates. Two lads were waiting and called him over. "Listen, you've got to do something for us. You've got to mark us in the register; we're going off for the day."

Freddie was shocked but the boys made it clear he had to do it "Or else!". Actually, it was quite easy, he thought as he ticked their names, nobody seemed to notice. The next morning it happened again. Freddie became scared, what if he got caught? He would be the one in trouble, but the boys kept threatening him. What could he do?

Story Worksheet

(Write or draw your answers)

1 Why was Freddie always so helpful? Did he have to do all those things at home and at school?

2 How do you think the two boys threatened him?

3 Would they have carried out their threats?

4 How could Freddie change the situation he is in?

Drama Worksheet

Warm-Ups & Drama Games

1 Choose a partner and hold a three-legged race without tying ankles together.

2 Trying walking a straight line with your eyes closed.

3 Choose a drama game from Appendix 3 for the whole group to play.

Exploration

a Suggest that everyone divides into groups of four and sets up a scene of Freddie doing everything that he is asked to do at home. Take turns in the role of Freddie.

b Set the scene where the two boys approach Freddie and threaten him if he doesn't do what they want.

c Suppose the teacher had seen the boys talking to Freddie, what might he have done? Set a scene with the teacher watching and reacting.

d Experiment with different ways in which Freddie can stand up for himself, at home and at school.

WolfWork 18

Colour the Wolf Picture and think about the theme of bullying or intimidation.

Write or draw your answers.

1 Why is this wolf being bullied?

2 Can the larger wolf stand up for itself?

3 Will other wolves come to help?

My Progress Today

1 I felt very angry when I was playing the part of:

Freddie ○   Intimidator 1 ○

Intimidator 2 ○   Teacher ○

2 I felt very unhappy when I was playing the part of:

Teacher ○   Freddie ○

Intimidator 1 ○   Intimidator 2 ○

3 I think the teacher should:

Punish the Intimidators ○

Be more aware of Freddie ○

Talk to the whole class ○

Understand more about intimidation ○

4 Draw a picture or describe how Freddie felt when being intimidated.

Homework

Things to think about …

1 Next time you see someone being intimidated think about what your own feelings might be.

2 What would you do if you were asked to do something that was wrong?

3 What sort of things might people try and force you to do?

(Discuss these questions with family and friends if you can.)

Bring your thoughts to the next session and draw or write a portrait of someone who intimidates others.

Session 5   Anger & Chaos

I am angry because I feel messed-up

Preparation & Resources: Discarded paperback books, scissors, white glue, thick felt-tip pens, large circles pre-drawn on blank sheets of paper.

Aim: To improve clarity and containment.

Focus: Discuss any thoughts and feelings from the previous session and share homework themes about intimidation.

Warm-Up: 'Pass the rhythm'; everyone sits in a circle, and one person claps a simple rhythm, then everyone claps it together; then in turn each person claps, clicks or stamps a rhythm that the group then copies.

Main Activities: Explain to the group that the paperback book will be a personalised book about themselves, and that pages can be cut out and replaced, or existing pages can be written over with felt-tip pens.

- Suggest each member of the group writes their name on one page and decorates that page with colours. Give the book the title 'My Journal' on another page, and decorate.

- Hand out the sheets of paper with circles on. Inside a circle each person should write two things that make them feel messed up, then cut the circle out and stick it inside their journal.

- Inside a second circle, write two questions that could help sort out the messed-up feelings, cut these out and stick them in journals.

More Advanced: In pairs, with a basic rule of no laughing or teasing, group members share one thing that they feel messes up their lives.

Feedback & Sharing: Discuss who might help people feel less messed up?

Closure: Decorate a page in 'My Journal' with patterns and symbols, while thinking about the themes discussed.

Read and discuss the story to finish or move on to the Story Worksheet or the Drama Exploration.

The Story

Darren just wanted some peace and quiet …

Darren lived in a house where there was always noise. His Dad worked on a building site and would come home after work, shouting for his dinner. His Mum worked in the supermarket and would come home very tired. His older sister was supposed to do the cooking because everyone was busy or tired and she would shout that it wasn't fair and she wanted to go out with her mates. Often Darren would help out in the kitchen himself just to keep the peace, although his Dad would shout that it was women's work and to leave them to it. Sometimes his Dad's mates would come round and call for him to go to the pub, which was great because everything was quiet for a while. At least it was until Dad came back drunk and shouting about anything and everything.

When the house was quiet, Darren would do his art; it wasn't just homework, it was work that he had developed himself. He really loved to draw the effect of the sun on buildings, trees and different objects. He shared his bedroom with his younger brother and had a pact with him not to mention the drawings and paintings. He just knew that his Dad wouldn't approve because he thought art was not a proper man's occupation and he knew his Mum would not approve because she couldn't wait for him to get a job and bring money into the house.

Soon there was going to be trouble because he had to decide about exams and maybe Art College.

Story Worksheet

(Write or draw your answers)

1 Which words would you use to describe all the noise in Darren's house?

2 Is there anyone in the house who might understand what he wants to do?

3 Should Darren forget his art and follow his dad onto the building site and do a 'proper man's job'?

4 Should he find any job he can and earn some money to help out his mum?

Drama Worksheet

Warm-Ups & Drama Games

1 Use the rhythm game from the Warm-Up but develop it standing up with claps, gestures, stamps, finger clicks and so on. Make sure everyone has a turn at making a rhythm for others to follow. Be aware that this could get competitive and possibly too complex!

2 Invite everyone to think about the different jobs on a building site and create scenes or sculpts of these in small groups.

3 Repeat the exercise with jobs in a supermarket.

Exploration of the Story

a In small groups create the noisy scene in Darren's house by using only sounds rather than words.

b Create a scene where Darren's younger brother gives his view of the situation.

c Have discussions about the roles and expectations of men and women and what they do. Then set up a 'debating society' that expresses traditional ideas and then more modern ideas.

d Continue the discussion but with group members 'in-role' as mum, dad, Darren and other members of the family.

 # WolfWork 19

Colour the Wolf picture and think about what is happening between these wolves: Who is close to whom?

Write or draw your answers.

1 Does the wolf on the ground want to escape?

2 Does the wolf really want to join the pack?

3 How might these wolves learn to trust each other?

My Progress Today

1 Draw a face in the circle to show how you are feeling today.

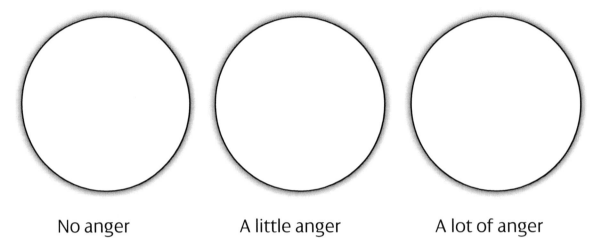

No anger   A little anger   A lot of anger

2 Using coloured pens, show in one of the circles how your muddles seem now.

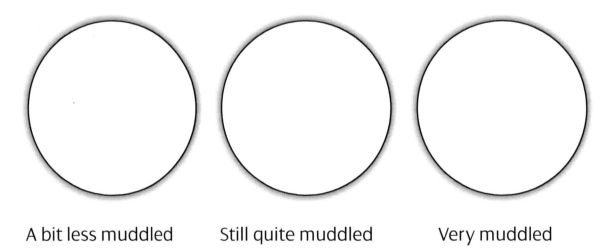

A bit less muddled   Still quite muddled   Very muddled

Homework

Things to think about – draw or write your thoughts.

1 What sorts of things are difficult if someone feels messed-up?

```



```

2 In what ways might we sort out confusions and messed-up feelings?

```



```

3 Is it OK to be different in some ways and not others?

```



```

Perhaps you can discuss these questions at home or with a friend who might have some ideas that could help.

Session 6   Anger & Fear

I am angry because I am frightened

Preparation & Resources: Folder, Personal Journals, white board, coloured markers, newspapers, magazines with plenty of pictures, scissors, glue, large sheets of plain paper.

Aim: To recognise angry feelings that can be triggered by fear.

Focus: Share thoughts and pictures from homework (feelings of being messed up), create a new page in Personal Journals called 'Colours of Fear'.

Warm-Up: Have a group discussion on the word 'fear': suggest that people focus on events that have been frightening and events that could be frightening, starting in a more general sense, for instance with items of world news (tsunamis, wars and so on) and encourage a gradual shift to more personal fears.

Main Activities: Invite everyone to think of words associated with fear and also physical feelings that accompany it (stomach churning or sweaty palms for example), and write these on the white board:

- Suggest everyone looks through newspapers and magazines and cuts out headlines or pictures of scary events.

- Link the fear words on white board with pictures of people who look scared, and match them up.

- In small groups create a collage of words and pictures that show fear.

- Share the collages and discuss similarities and differences.

More Advanced: Share with a partner something that is personally scary. Remind everyone of the Ground Rules first.

Feedback & Sharing: Encourage a discussion in the group of types of fear that can lead to anger and possible solutions (exploring the fear, asking questions, deep breathing).

Closure: Practise deep breathing exercises (see introduction, and Appendix 3) for calming and focussing, and even counting to 10! Write or draw in Personal Journals to finish the session or move on to Story and Drama Worksheets.

The Story

Pictures tell stories

Discuss within the group the idea that 'every picture tells a story'. Look at the collages you have made and then choose a story that one picture suggests. Write or draw the answers to the questions.

1 Who is in this story?

2 Why are they scared?

3 What can they do about it?

4 What will happen in the end?

Drama Worksheet

Warm-Ups & Drama Games

1 Invite everyone to run round the room as if they are jogging, then change to competing in a race, then to rushing for a train or bus, and finally to escaping from an attack.

2 In pairs improvise a scene in which a student is asked to go the head-teacher's office.

The teacher's aim: to tell the student some bad news from home.

The student's aim: to avoid being told off for fighting.

3 Create a group story without using words called 'breaking bad news'.

Exploration

a Either look at the collages and create a scene that is suggested by one of the pictures and create an ending to the scene.

b Using the 'breaking bad news' from the warm-up, develop the ideas to show how often we can be scared of receiving some news, and it then turns out to be OK.

WolfWork 20

Colour the Wolf Picture and think about why this wolf is so frightened?

Write or draw your answers.

1 How do we know this wolf is frightened?

2 What could help the wolf to feel more relaxed?

3 Can this wolf find a partner?

My Progress Today

Understanding my fears: colour in the circle which best shows how you are feeling.

I understand my fears a lot more than before.

I understand my fears a little more than before.

I still feel fearful.

'I still feel scared about …': (Write or draw a picture to explain your feelings.)

Homework

Things to think about …

1 What does my body signal when I am scared?

```
[                                                              ]
```

2 Who can I tell about being scared?

```
[                                                              ]
```

3 Can I help someone else who is scared?

```
[                                                              ]
```

Discuss these ideas with family and friends if possible.

Write down some words or draw a picture on the theme of fear and anger.

```
[                                                              ]
```

Session 7 Anger & Resolution

Integrating all the sessions

Preparation & Resources: Make sure all of the resources that have been used during the seven sessions are available, including a circle of chairs, the group's folders and Personal Journals.

Aim: To bring together the various themes of the programme and to look at people's progress throughout.

Focus: Invite everyone to bring thoughts and feelings from the previous session and share any pictures they have created.

Warm-Up: Suggest that everyone starts off in the circle and talks about their 'journey through the course'. Place seven chairs in a row, with spaces between them, and invite group members to sit in one chair at a time and make a statement using either words or gestures, or both, about what they learned in that week.

Main Activities: Invite everyone to look through their folders and share with a partner:

- The things they found most difficult.

- Their struggles and achievements during the course.

- Something they still need to watch out for.

Invite group members to give feedback to others.

Now invite people to choose a favourite physical activity to repeat. Finally, celebrate everyone's sense of achievement with what they have accomplished.

More Advanced: Suggest that people tell their partner what their worst fear was when they first joined the group.

Feedback & Sharing: Invite comments and feedback from everyone.

Closure: Invite individuals to write or draw a closing entry in their Personal Journal, continue to the Story and Drama Worksheets and the WolfWork, finally present the Certificates.

The Story

Hephaestus: The God of blacksmiths & metal workers

Hephaestus was born to Zeus and Hera, and immediately Zeus could see that he had a deformed leg and would always be lame. He and Hera were appalled at this so Zeus took the child by his ankle, swung him around his head, and threw him as far as possible into the sea, thinking that would be the end of him. However, the baby was found by two sea nymphs who immediately decided to care for him and placed him safely in an underground cave.

As he grew up, Hephaestus began to work with metals and precious jewels, and he had an underground furnace in the cave where he developed his craft. Soon he became famous for his skills and people would order exquisite jewellery and metal work from him. However, he remained very, very angry with his parents, especially with his mother for neglecting him.

He decided he would take revenge on her and created the most beautiful, magical chair ever seen, encrusted with precious stones. He invited his mother to a celebration and presented her with the chair; she sat down and immediately locks snapped round her wrists and ankles, trapping her. She screamed to be released but Hephaestus laughed and laughed. Even Zeus, his estranged father could not persuade him to release Hera.

Eventually, Dionysus, the god of wine-making, took him for a chat and a mug of wine. After Dionysus listened to his troubled story, he suggested to Hephaestus that he had at last shown his mother how angry he was. Hephaestus agreed on the condition that his mother would help him find a very beautiful wife, which she did. But that is another story …

Story Worksheet

This is a very old story from ancient Greece. Think about the themes that are still relevant today: rejection, anger and feelings of revenge.

1 What is the strongest feeling in this story and how is it expressed?

2 Why did Hephaestus' parent reject him?

3 How was he able to concentrate on being such a good craftsman?

4 Do you agree with the ending of this story?

Drama Worksheet

Warm-Ups & Drama Games

1 Invite everyone to imagine they have been thrown into the sea and are swimming for survival.

2 Using enormous hammers, beat a sheet of metal into shape to create something useful.

3 With very fine and delicate movements create shapes and patterns of jewels to wear.

Exploration of the Story

a Ask the group to divide into pairs and to imagine they have found a small abandoned baby, and discuss what they might do.

b With the whole group, create the scene where Hera is invited to the presentation of the chair. Everyone must react to what has happened.

c In pairs create the scene with Hephaestus and Dionysus where one is telling the story and the other is giving advice.

d Share the scenes with the whole group.

WolfWork 21

Colour the Wolf Picture and think about how relaxed these two wolves seem to be.

Write or draw your answers

1 What do you think the relationship is between these wolves?

2 How have they achieved the calm between them?

3 Can you identify with these feelings?

What I have achieved on this course

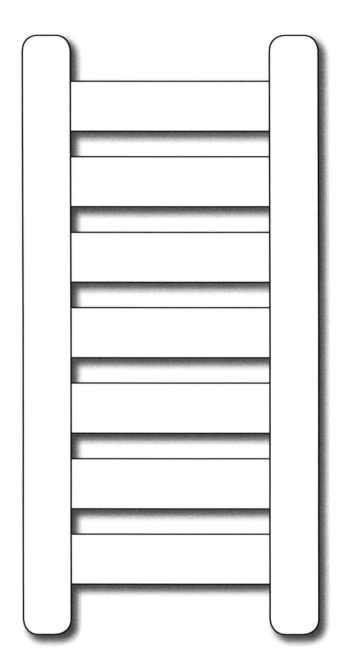

1 Fill in each step of the ladder with something that you have achieved during the seven weeks of the course.

2 What was the most difficult step to climb to?

3 Did you have any doubts that you would make it?

4 Congratulate yourself on your achievements and accept the Certificate when it is presented to you and be proud of it!

Part 4

Resources

Progress Sheet 1:
The Face of My Anger

1 Colour in the face that shows how you are feeling now.

Not angry at all   A little bit angry   very angry

2 Have you ever felt angry because you feel different? Colour the circle to show how different you feel from other people.

      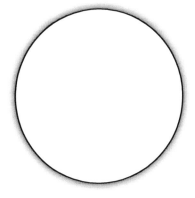

Very different   Quite different   A little different

Progress Sheet 2:
The Fire of My Anger

1 Colour the fire to show whether you were feeling lots of anger, some anger or only a little anger when you started today.

2 By the end of the session were you feeling:

 A bit more angry than usual?

 A bit less angry than usual?

 Just the same?

3 Do you enjoy watching fires?

Progress Sheet 3:
The Sound of My Anger

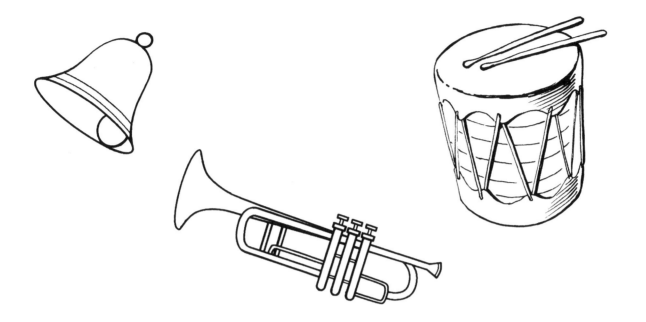

1 Which of these instruments would you play to show how you are feeling now? Colour your choice in with colours that you like.

2 Draw a cross on the line to show where you feel your anger is right now.

_____

Very Angry   Quite Angry   Little Angry

3 How did you feel about Robin and his being teased and bullied?

Progress Sheet 4:
The Claws of My Anger

1 Colour in the tiger to show whether you were feeling lots of anger, some anger or a little anger today.

2 Colour in the circle of how you are feeling right now.

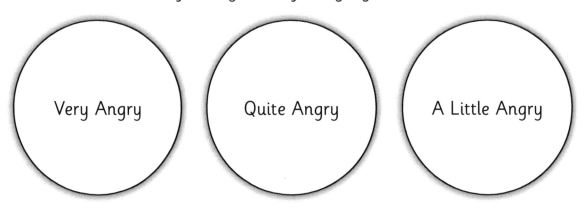

Very Angry   Quite Angry   A Little Angry

3 What did you feel about how the bandits treated the tiger to make her angry?

Progress Sheet 5:
The Smoke of My Anger

1 Colour in the dragon to show if you were feeling lots of anger, some anger or a little anger today.

2 By the end of the session were you feeling:

 A bit more angry than usual?

 A bit less angry than usual?

 Just the same?

Progress Sheet 6:
The Teeth of My Anger

1 Colour the shark to show how you are feeling: very angry, quite angry or a little angry.

2 By the end of the session were you feeling:

 A bit more angry than usual?

 A bit less angry than usual?

 Just the same?

3 How do you think Greatly was feeling during the storm? Scared? Angry? Lost?

Progress Sheet 7:
The Steps I Have Achieved

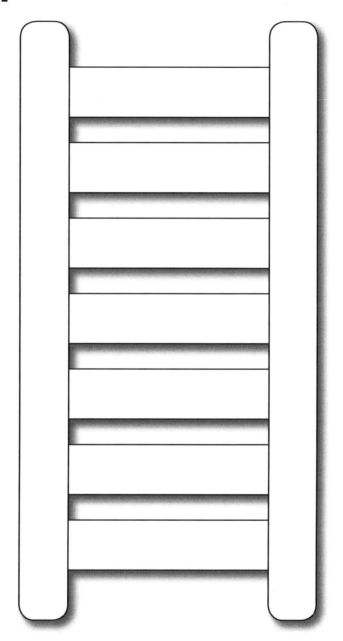

1 At the top of the ladder write your personal goal that you hope to achieve by the end of the seven group sessions.

2 Write on the bottom rung what you think you have achieved in the first session.

3 Write below what you think the most difficult task will be during the course.

Progress Sheet 8: My Anger Erupts

1 Colour the volcano to show whether you were feeling lots of anger, some anger or only a little anger today.

2 By the end of the session were you feeling:

☐   A bit more angry than usual?

☐   A bit less angry than usual?

☐   Just the same?

3 Do you enjoy watching fire? What does it make you feel?

Progress Sheet 9:
My Anger Started Sadly

1 Colour the Meerkat to show how you were feeling: lots of anger, some anger or a little anger today.

2 By the end of the session were you feeling:

 A bit more angry than usual?

 A bit less angry than usual?

 Just the same?

3 What advice would you give to Millie to stop her becoming so unhappy?

Progress Sheet 10:
My Anger is Prickly

Which of the roses would you choose to show how you are feeling?
Colour it in.

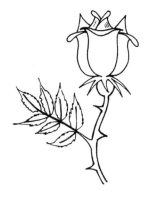

Lots of thorns?

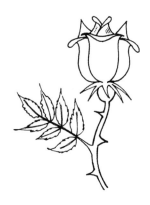

A few thorns?

One or two thorns?

Worksheet 1

Ground Rules for the Group

Ground Rules can discussed with group members at a preliminary meeting or at the first session. The Group Facilitator needs to be clear on the basic rules that are non-negotiable. For example, people are not to be hurt physically or verbally. There is zero tolerance of bullying. Any equipment used is to be respected.

The group are likely to make their own suggestions about people 'mucking about' (not listening to each other); 'taking control' (intimidating each other), 'ganging up on each other', 'staying in the room'. Allow as much democracy as possible, but ensure you have the final vote.

Rules can then be written out and stuck on the wall during group sessions.

A sample set of rules could be as follows:

GROUND RULES FOR THE ANGER MANAGEMENT GROUP

Dates: _____ to _____

The group agrees the following:

1 No-one hurts or bullies anyone else.

2 Everyone listens when others are speaking.

3 When the teacher or leader calls "Freeze!" everyone must stop and listen.

4 Everyone must stay in the room until the end of the session.

Signed by the Group:

_____   _____

_____   _____

_____   _____

Worksheet 2

Contract for Group Members

CONTRACT

This is the Agreement between

_____

(participant's name)

and

_____

(group leader's name)

for the

Anger Management Project

Dates _____

Ground Rules

1 Nobody gets hurt either physically or verbally

2 No property gets damaged

3 Everyone listens to everyone else

4 Everyone respects the others in the group

5 Everyone tries to be on time and to attend every session

6 Another rule from the group?

Signed by Participant _____

Signed by Group Leader _____

Worksheet 3

Angry Words

Annoyed

Irritated

MAD

ANGRY

Cross

FURIOUS

crazy

BOILING

Add angry expressions that you can think of in the space below and add angry colours too:

Worksheet 4

Diary Notes

Diary notes can be written or drawn at the end of every session. The notes can include what you liked about the session, what you did not like, anything you felt was an improvement ... or they can be just about how you are feeling.

Write or draw in the boxes.

How am I feeling?

What was not so good today?

What was good today?

What questions do I not like people asking me?

Write or draw any other thoughts on the session?

Worksheet 5

Teenage Rap
'Don't Talk To Me'

Don't touch me

Don't talk to me

I don't need your empathy

Just leave me alone

Just let me be angry

You don't know what it's like to be me

You don't know the red mist I see

You don't know the clenched fist when your head's a mess

You don't know what to do when there are no words left

My mouth can't speak

But my body roars

It's a weapon of mass destruction

It's a raging inner war

from the **Actionwork Project**

Worksheet 6

My Anger Thermometer

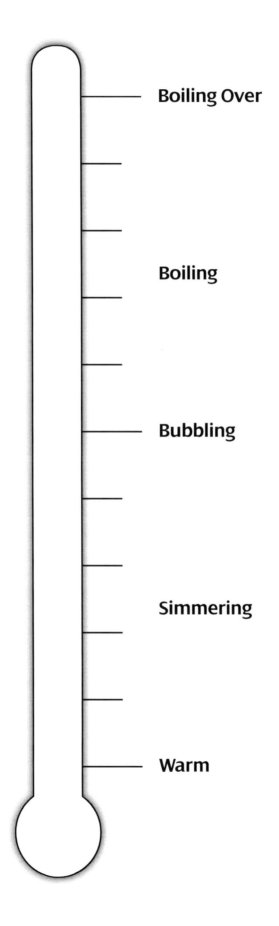

Boiling Over

Boiling

Bubbling

Simmering

Warm

Worksheet 7

The Worry Scale

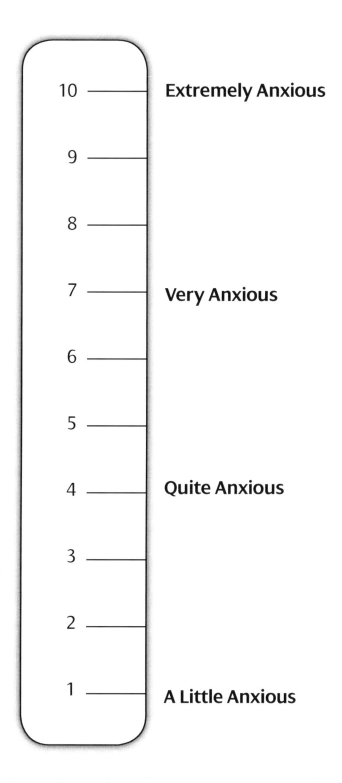

10 ——— **Extremely Anxious**

9 ———

8 ———

7 ——— **Very Anxious**

6 ———

5 ———

4 ——— **Quite Anxious**

3 ———

2 ———

1 ——— **A Little Anxious**

1 Colour in the scale to show how anxious you are feeling most of the time.

2 Write or draw what makes you worried by the side of the scale.

Worksheet 8

My Worries & Anxieties

1 What makes you feel anxious?

Worries about the family ☐

Worries about school work ☐

Worries about health ☐

Worries about what other people think ☐

Something else ☐

Write what it is here if you wish: _____

2 What happens when you are anxious or worried?

Can't get to sleep ☐

Can't concentrate at school ☐

Always tired ☐

Irritable to other people ☐

Bite nails ☐

Something else ☐

Write what it is here if you wish: _____

3 What could help your worries?

Someone to talk to ☐

Someone to give me information ☐

Someone to do something about ☐

Something else ☐

Write what it is if you wish: _____

4 Today I am going to try and overcome my worries by:

(Write or draw what it could be)

Worksheet 9

Triggers for my Anger 1

This Worksheet is to see what triggers your anger (a) and how you react (b), how your anger activates (c), and how it can de-activate (d). For example the trigger could be that someone has spoilt your homework (a), you react by tensing up all through your body (b), you activate it by shouting and swearing very loudly (c), and often someone else will de-activate it by punishing you or shouting at you (d).

Sample Trigger Worksheet

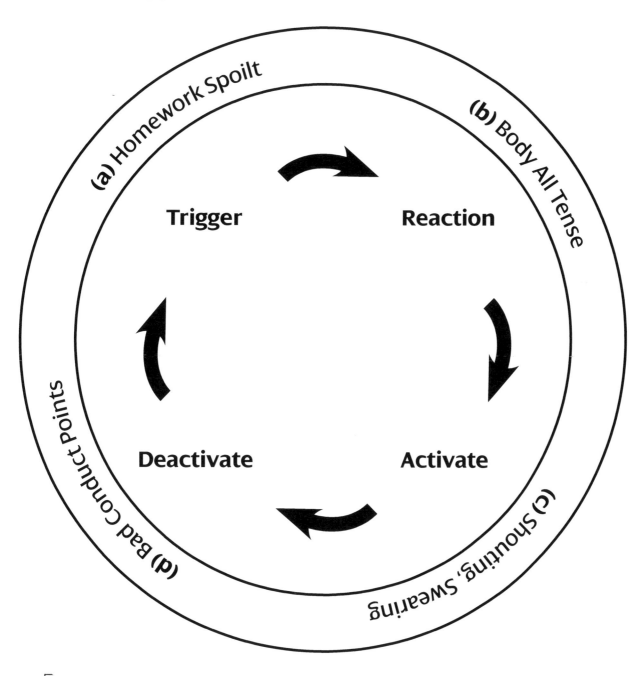

Worksheet 10

Triggers for my Anger 2

This Worksheet is to see what triggers your anger (a) and how you react.

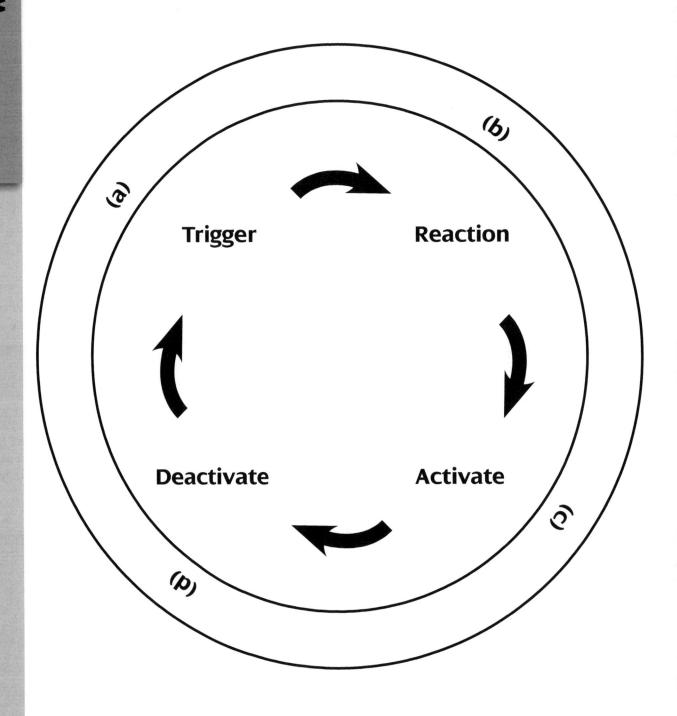

Worksheet 11

Why are People Intimidated?

Being intimidated is more than just being scared; if someone intimidates us we can feel sweaty or our stomach can thump or we can feel cold or have other physical reactions.

We can have a feeling of dread which can stop us from doing things such as leaving the house, meeting relatives or going to school or other places.

Write down reasons why someone might feel intimidated:

List some feelings you might have if someone intimidates you:

Draw a picture of a place where you feel intimidated:

Draw a funny cartoon picture of a person who intimidates you:

Try and remember this cartoon next time you feel scared of this person.

Remember that people who intimidate others often feel very scared themselves underneath!

Worksheet 12

How I Am Feeling Today

Today I feel I can understand my angry feelings: colour in the apple to show your understanding.

I can understand my feelings a lot.

I can understand my feelings a bit.

I can understand my feelings a little.

Worksheet 13a

The Story: Jamie the New Boy

Jamie came from a different school in a remote place in the north of Scotland. His dad had a new job in England, much further south than he had ever been before. When they moved to their new house the first thing he noticed was that everything was so green. He had been used to the heather and the hills, plenty of snow and not a lot of sunshine.

When Jamie started his new school, he stayed fairly quiet, he wasn't shy but was a boy of few words. At twelve years old he was quite independent and used to looking after himself. The other kids in his class were reasonably friendly, but they weren't too sure of this new boy with the Scottish accent.

Most people at school brought their own lunches. Lots of people had crisps, chocolate bars and fizzy drinks; others had packed lunches made by their mums or dads. Jamie always bought a thick sandwich made from home-made bread with a large piece of cheese and an apple. He never had fizzy drinks but had a drink of water from the drinking fountain instead.

Gradually some of the other kids in the class decided that Jamie was weird: he was different in so many ways: what he ate, how he talked – when he did! Yes, he was definitely different and … weird.

Story Worksheet 13b

Jamie the New Boy

1 What was different about Jamie that made others think he was weird?

2 Would the other pupils say anything to him about being different?

3 If they mocked him for being different, how do you think Jamie would respond?

Drama Worksheet 13c

Jamie the New Boy

Warm-Ups & Drama Games

1 Ask everyone to walk round the room with an exaggerated walk, as silly as they can; then add arm gestures as large as possible; greet everyone else in an 'over the top' way with bows or curtseys or huge waves and so on.

2 Suggest everyone finds a partner and chooses a role: e.g., builder, cook, duchess or duke, doctor. The pairs must interact using exaggerated voices and gestures.

3 Now experiment with saying things which are not what their characters would usually say: for example, the duchess says to the doctor, "I hear you have problems with a leaking roof, fetch me a ladder …"

Exploration of the Story

a Continue working in pairs, with one person saying all the things (note: these are imagined) that are weird about their partner, then change over.

b Suggest that everyone forms small groups and think about the story of Jamie; then create a scene where one or two people start to call him weird, different and so on. The group must decide together how Jamie deals with it.

c Invite the group to imagine that Jamie writes a journal when he gets home: create a scene where one person is Jamie and the others act out what he is writing.

d Share scenes with other group members and discuss times when feeling different can make us feel angry.

Worksheet 14

Certificate

awarded to

_____

for attending the

Anger Management Project

and showing changes in

1 _____

2 _____

3 _____

Signed _____
Project Leader

Date _____

APPENDIX 3
Drama Games & Warm-Ups

Warm-Ups

It is important when choosing warm-ups that they are linked to the activities in the group and not chosen at random. A warm-up is just that, it warms up the body and the brain, ready for creative activity.

I start with physical warm-ups because often there is surplus energy that needs to be focussed and then transformed. My approach does not work with angry expression for its own sake, with activities such as smashing old china or breaking bricks, I use physical energy that expresses angry energy and then turns it into something else.

For example, a physical game of throwing and catching a soft ball, focuses scattered energy and allows it to become collaborative energy. A jog around the park or playing field encourages a 'feel good' factor and prepares group members for focussed group work.

In all warm-ups it is important to keep an awareness of breathing, whether to create energy or to bring about relaxation.

Breathing & Voice

These exercises should be repeated 3 or 4 times.

1 Breathe in through the nose to a count of 4 and out through the mouth to a count of 4, ensure the shoulders are relaxed and the tummy tucked in. Repeat with a pause for 4 counts between breathing in and out.

2 Take a deep breath in through the nose, and breath out on the word 'Home'.

3 Say the phrase, 'Ho, Ho, Ho' as loud as possible; repeat getting louder, then repeat getting softer.

4 Repeat quickly: 'Red leather-Yellow leather', first 5 times, then 10 times.

5 Repeat quickly: 'A clown with a crown', first 5 times, then 10 times.

6 Talk in a nonsense language with a partner as fast as possible, and then very slowly as if feeling sleepy.

Physical

1 Throw a soft ball to each other while on the run round the room or field; vary with throwing the ball and shouting names.

2 Hold hands in a circle and pull first one way and then the other and keep the circle intact.

3 Hold hands in a circle and move over and under everyone until a tight knot is formed. Slowly undo the knot without letting go of any hands.

4 Pass a clap or a rhythm around the circle to create a ripple effect as if it is continuous.

5 Stand in a circle, at a signal each person needs to sit down – but only one at a time! If two people sit down at the same time, then start again from the beginning. Repeat the exercise but with standing up from a sitting position.

Drama Games

1 Choose partners and hold a three-legged race without tying ankles together.

2 Create Stepping Stones across the room with pieces of newspaper. Everyone needs to cross the 'river' or 'chasm' without tearing the paper; elaborate with two people having to work together and move on each piece of paper.

3 The group pretend they are medical students at a lecture and someone has come to give them a talk on knitting.

4 The group pretend they are housewives and househusbands, and someone has come to give them a talk on brain surgery.

5   Two people are fruit and vegetable stall holders and call out what they are selling along with the prices; they must try to compete with each other in both price and volume!

6   In pairs, one person is a customer and the other a salesman trying to show all the best points of a car, but not knowing anything about cars so they try to bluff their way through the discussion.

7   In pairs, one person is a student and the other a physics teacher giving a lecture, but really they are a piano teacher and know nothing about physics.

8   In small groups, one person leads the others across different terrains such as desert, rain forest, ice flows, streams, farm yard. Group members don't know what the terrain is so they must follow and copy and then guess at the end.

9   Repeat but with the setting being ice that is about to crack or a landslide about to give way so everyone has to move quickly and lightly.

All of these exercises can be developed into extended situations or stories.

Body Sculpts

There are several ways of creating body sculpts and they are useful for creating an instant image, sometimes called a 'freeze frame'. Group members can be asked to 'freeze' in a particular shape (tall, round, wide and so on) or a mood (e.g., scared, angry, excited). Working in pairs one person can sculpt the other in a shape or mood or character.

The whole group can work together to 'build' a sculpt that represents success or difficulties or celebration.

Group members can also be invited to sculpt a story in small sub-groups, especially if they are anxious about drama work: one sculpt to represent the beginning of the story, one for the middle and one for the end. This technique can be used for personal stories of events or for particular fairy tales or myths.

APPENDIX 4
Useful Reading

Drost J. 2011, *Promoting Friendship, Emotional & Social Skills in Children: The Giant's Desk*, Hinton House Publishers, Buckingham.

Hickson A. 2011, *How to Stop Bullying: 101 Strategies that really work*, Speechmark, Milton Keynes.

Jennings S. 2010, *StoryBuilding 100+ Ideas for Developing Story and Narrative Skills*, Hinton House Publishers, Buckingham.

———— 2011, *101 Activities for Empathy & Awareness*, Hinton House Publishers, Buckingham.

———— 2012, *101 Activities for Managing Challenging Behaviour*, Hinton House Publishers, Buckingham.

Johnston C. 2010, *Drama Games for those who like to say no.* Nick Hern Books, London.

Portmann R. 2008, *The 50 Best Games for Building Self-Esteem*, Hinton House Publishers, Buckingham.

Sunderland M. 2003, *Helping Children Locked in Rage or Hate*, Speechmark, Milton Keynes.

———— 2008, *Smasher: A story to help teenagers with anger & alienation*, Hinton House Publishers, Buckingham.

———— 2012, *Helping Teenagers with Anger, Alienation & Low Self-Esteem*, Hinton House Publishers, Buckingham.

Swale J. 2009, *Drama Games for Classrooms and Workshops*, Nick Hern Books, London.

Thomas B. 2011, *Creative Expressive Activities for Teens. Jessica Kingsley Publishers*, London.

www.suejennings.com

www.actionwork.com

www.dramatherapy.net

www.antiviolencecampus.org